grilling
new healthy kitchen

RECIPES

Annabel Langbein

GENERAL EDITOR

Chuck Williams

PHOTOGRAPHY

Dan Goldberg

Bonnier
Books

contents

Introduction

8   Eating the rainbow

10   The new healthy kitchen

12   Fruits & vegetables

13   Grains & legumes

14   All about grilling

16   Creating the healthy meal

18 Purple & blue

23   Grilled aubergine & feta cheese rolls

     Scallops with pepper dressing

24   Grilled pizzas with blue potatoes & onions

27   Fig & purple endive salad

     Halibut & purple grapes

30   Grilled salmon with purple asparagus slaw

33   Chicken, aubergine & tomato salad

     Chicken & fig kebabs

34   Grilled plums with kirsch cream

     Grilled berry parcels

36 Green

41   Belgian endive with blue cheese & walnuts

     Spring onions with anchovy sauce

42   Grilled fish tacos with green cabbage salad

45   Trout & green pear salad

     Grilled halibut with limes

48   Chicken, avocado & spinach salad

     Green & yellow beans with almonds

51   Lamb chops with rocket pesto

     Broccoli gratin

52   Grilled apple hotcakes

54 White & tan

59   Mushroom bruschetta

     Mustard-honey leeks

60   Turkey sandwiches with sweet onions

     Grilled white corn salad

63   Grilled lobster tails with white corn salsa

66   Cuban-style pork & plantains

69   White aubergine & spring onion salad

     Grilled fennel with indian spices

70   White nectarine kebabs

Reference

126 Nutrients at work

130 Nutritional values

134 Glossary

139 Bibliography

140 Index

144 Acknowledgements

72 Yellow & orange

77 Yellow tomatoes with mint & pecorino

Grilled pumpkin with pumpkin
seed dressing

78 Grilled salmon, potato
& corn salad

81 Grilled duck breast with papaya

84 Grilled snapper & mandarin salad

Mahimahi with mango salsa

87 Japanese-style grilled sweet potatoes

Grilled crookneck squash salad

88 Grilled apricots with sabayon

90 Red

95 Radicchio with balsamic glaze

Liver & onion bruschetta

96 Grilled calamari

Romesco sauce

99 Prawns with watermelon, feta & mint

Grilled cherry tomatoes

102 Lamb kebabs with blood orange salad

105 Veal chops with red plum sauce

Chicken with cherry salsa

106 Caramelised red pears with cinnamon

Grilled grapes in yoghurt & sour cream

108 Brown

113 Grilled polenta with mushroom ragout

114 Chicken thighs with lima bean purée

117 Grilled tuna with cannellini bean salad

120 Pepper & quinoa salad

123 Bulgur salad with courgette, asparagus
& spring onions

124 Grilled bananas with nuts & chocolate

About this book

This volume of the New Healthy Kitchen was created to show how grilling can be a simple and appealing way to prepare nutrient-rich fruits, vegetables, legumes and grains as well as lean meats, poultry and seafood.

Today, we have a multitude of choices when it comes to food, from locally grown fruits and vegetables to a vast array of processed convenience items. With so many options comes a responsibility to choose wisely and well. It's a proven fact that the foods you eat directly affect your overall health and energy levels. One of the best ways you can ensure you experience the benefits of both is to add plenty of fresh produce and whole grains to your diet.

The recipes in *Grilling* are organised in a new way: by the colour of the key fruits or vegetables used in the dish. This approach highlights the different nutritional benefits that each colour group contributes to your overall health. By thinking about the colour of foods, you can be sure to include all the fresh produce you need in your diet. If you consume at least one vegetable or fruit from each colour group daily, you can feel confident you are getting the number of servings required for optimum health. Whole grains and legumes have a chapter of their own and, like fresh produce, form the foundation of a wholesome diet.

The New Healthy Kitchen series will help you prepare a wide range of fresh fruits, vegetables and whole grains using different healthy cooking techniques, bringing colour to every meal you make.

Chuck Williams

Eating the rainbow

Purple and blue fruits and vegetables contain fibre, vitamins and phytochemicals that promote heart health; help memory function; lower the risk of some cancers; promote urinary tract health; and boost immunity

Green fruits and vegetables contain fibre, vitamins and phytochemicals that lower the risk of breast, prostate, lung and other cancers; promote eye health; help build strong bones and teeth; and boost immunity

White and tan fruits and vegetables contain fibre, vitamins and phytochemicals that promote heart health; help maintain healthful cholesterol levels; lower the risk of breast, lung, and other cancers; and slow cholesterol absorption

Red fruits and vegetables contain fibre, vitamins and phytochemicals that promote heart health; help memory function; lower the risk of certain cancers; promote urinary tract health; and boost immunity

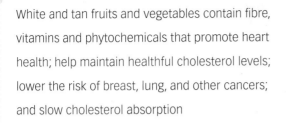

Yellow and orange fruits and vegetables contain fibre, vitamins and phytochemicals that promote heart health; promote eye health; lower the risk of some cancers; and boost immunity

Brown whole grains, legumes, seeds and nuts include fibre, vitamins and phytonutrients that lower blood cholesterol levels and reduce the risk of colon and other cancers, diabetes, heart disease and stroke

Adapted from educational materials of the Produce for Better Health Foundation

The new healthy kitchen

Initially, a cookbook organised by colour that promotes a healthy diet sounds like a questionable idea. Focusing on the red of tomatoes or the yellow of squash seems like a distraction when you are trying to cut out "bad" foods and fill up on "good" ones on your path to healthier eating. But in fact, the best and most natural way to improve your diet is to start thinking about the colours on your plate.

The philosophy of the New Healthy Kitchen series is simple and straightforward: the consumption of moderate amounts of a wide range of foods, especially peak-of-season produce and whole or minimally processed grains, is the key to a healthy diet. Instead of counting calories, fat grams, or carbohydrates, you need to focus on maintaining a constantly varied diet rich in fresh vegetables, fruits, grains and legumes. If consuming such foods is the first priority of your daily regimen, a healthier balance of other foods will naturally follow.

The modern diet is remarkably restricted in the kind of plant foods people eat. Instead of having to forage for our next meal, we are able to surround ourselves with every possible food luxury—and it's hard not to overindulge in concentrated sources of energy, especially animal fats. Our appetites gravitate toward carbohydrates, which are excellent sources of quick energy. Unfortunately, our most common forms of carbohydrates, such as white bread and white rice, are stripped of the wholesome nutrients found in whole grains.

While taking a daily multivitamin is a practical insurance policy, popping pills and supplements isn't a good solution to an ongoing lack of vitamins and minerals

in your diet. Your body can make better use of these compounds when it extracts them in their natural state from food. Eating a wide variety of plant foods, rounded out with a bit of meat and seafood, is the best way of getting what you need, in a form in which your body is designed to use it.

The colours of these plant foods are an important part of the equation. Some of the benefits of eating fruits and vegetables come from the vitamins, minerals and fibre they contain, but others come from a newly discovered class of nutrients called phytonutrients or phytochemicals. These plant compounds work in a number of ways to protect our bodies and fight disease. In many cases, they are also the elements in plant foods that give them their distinctive colours and flavours. So the dazzling hues of vegetables and fruits, from bright red tomatoes to dark green spinach to deep purple aubergine, give clues to the particular phytonutrients each plant contains. Eating a rainbow of produce will give you the broadest array of health benefits from all these various nutrients.

But these colourful fruits and vegetables are not the only elements of a sound regimen. Your daily diet must also include members of another important group of plant foods, grains and legumes, all of which are rich in fibre, protein, complex carbohydrates and minerals, as well as phytochemicals of their own. For the greatest nutritional benefit, the grains must be eaten whole or only minimally processed.

This volume of the New Healthy Kitchen series offers ways to enjoy this wholesome natural bounty using one of the oldest and most healthy cooking methods: grilling. Cooking foods over a fire brings out their natural flavours and, at the same time, gently imbues them with a smoky taste that appeals to nearly every palate.

To guide your meal planning, the chapters in this cookbook are organised by the five prominent colour groups of vegetables and fruits: purple and blue, green, white and tan, yellow and orange, and red. A sixth chapter focuses on "brown" foods, including whole grains, legumes, nuts and seeds. Focusing on this rainbow of colour will put a wealth of new or passed-over healthy—and very flavoursome—foods on your daily table.

Fruits & vegetables

Fruits and vegetables are the cornerstone of a healthy diet. They are also some of the most beautiful and delicious foods on the planet—a boon to both the eye and the palate, with tastes and textures that range from sweet, juicy peaches to bitter, crisp radicchio. The recipes in *Grilling* will inspire you to try new fruits and vegetables and reap the benefits of their vitamins, minerals and phytochemicals.

In the early years of the twentieth century, scientists discovered, one by one, the many different vitamins and minerals we now know are essential to maintaining good health and fighting disease. Today, we are entering into a similarly exciting era of discovery as we learn about the roles that phytonutrients play in our bodies.

These protective compounds, which are believed to number in the thousands, work alone and in combination with one another and with nutrients. They work in different ways. For example, some phytochemicals act as antioxidants, protecting the body by neutralising unstable oxygen molecules (known as free radicals) that damage cells and promote disease. Regularly eating plant foods rich in antioxidants can reduce the incidence of various cancers, heart disease, impaired vision and other health problems.

Fruits and vegetables from different colour groups provide us with different assortments of phytonutrients, each playing a unique role in fighting disease and promoting health and well-being.

By eating fruits and vegetables at their peak of ripeness, you will be both pleasing your palate and giving your body the benefit of all the healthy nutrients that these plant foods contain.

Grains & legumes

Grains and legumes have long played key roles in the human diet. In Asia, a meal is not a meal without rice, while beans are seldom absent from the Mexican table. British diners are accustomed to eating white rice or a white bread roll as part of dinner, but not venturing beyond these familiar items. Lately, however, more interest has risen in healthier whole grains, from nutty brown rice to exotic amaranth.

Perhaps the interest comes in reaction to the promotion of low-carbohydrate diets, which made white breads and pastas taboo. Whatever the cause of this trend, making a shift from refined white grains to unrefined brown ones is a welcome development for everyone's health.

Whole grains and legumes are good sources of fibre, which keeps our digestive system in good working order and helps regulate the cholesterol levels in our blood. They also contain many proteins, vitamins, minerals and their own phytochemicals. But in our modern diet, grains are usually refined, with the fibre-rich hull and the nutrient-rich germ removed.

In the New Healthy Kitchen, recipes that feature grains and legumes are grouped in a chapter called Brown. These foods come in a variety of colours, but you should think of them as brown to remind yourself that they should be as close to their natural state as possible, rather than stripped of nutrients, texture, flavour and colour.

The recipes in this book encourage you to try a variety of grains, such as bulgur and rice, in their whole forms. It is worthwhile experimenting with other, less common whole grains, too, such as quinoa, an ancient South American grain.

Legumes, which are the seeds of plants that split open when dried, include peas,

beans, lentils and peanuts. They contain fibre, complex carbohydrates, phosphorus and iron, plus plenty of protein: 50g (2oz) cooked dried beans or 1 tablespoon peanut butter equals 25g (1oz) of cooked meat, fish or poultry. And they are available in a wide range of appealing colours and shapes, from yellow chickpeas and green split peas to red, green, yellow, brown and tiny black lentils.

Seeds belonging to this same category include flaxseed, sesame seeds, and all types of tree nuts, from almonds to walnuts. These are rich in omega-3 fatty acids and high in fibre, which has been shown to help keep cholesterol levels down. Nuts are also a good source of heart-healthy vitamin E.

All about grilling

Whether the product of a happy accident or clever invention, grilling is the oldest cooking method. There is a primal satisfaction in preparing food over an open flame that is difficult to find in any other cooking technique. We have refined the method over the centuries, with the use of grills, racks, charcoal and now gas grills, but the essential spirit of grilling remains the same.

Most people associate grilling with warm summer weather, and this is often one of the best parts of the experience: cooking and eating in the open air. However, the advent of the popular gas grill has made cold-weather grilling more widely possible. It's a time-saver, too, eliminating the time needed to prepare the coals.

Even during the most inclement weather, however, remember that you have another option: your grill. While it does not impart the same smoky flavour, it does cook foods quickly using high heat, and almost any grilling recipe can be adapted to the grill. Moving the racks closer to or farther away from the heat element gives you the same

type of control as arranging coals in a kettle grill or turning the knobs of a gas grill.

The recipes in this volume take a straightforward approach: most call for direct grilling over medium heat. The heat level is a little lower than in some grilling cookbooks, in the interest of keeping the recipes as healthy as possible. When meat is cooked at high temperatures over hot coals, carcinogens are created both by an amino acid reaction in the food and by fat dripping onto the coals and releasing smoke.

You will want a chimney starter to set up a charcoal grill. This simple contraption allows you to light coals without using chemicals. The coals burn in the chimney until they are covered with white ash, at which point you spread them evenly over the bottom of the grill. It is useful to leave a section of the grill empty of coals to create a cooler area, so that if flare-ups occur, you can move the food to the cooler area temporarily. If you want to grill food over an indirect fire, set the food over the empty area and close the lid of the grill to create an ovenlike environment.

To test the accurate temperature level of a charcoal grill, hold your hand about 10 cm (4 in) above the coals and count the number of seconds you can keep it there comfortably: 1 to 2 seconds indicates a hot fire, 3 to 4 seconds indicates a medium fire, and 5 seconds or more is a low fire. You can also use an oven thermometer, with the grill lid in place, to test the correct temperature, given in the recipes.

Using a gas grill for direct grilling is simple: turn the knobs to light the burner(s) the food will sit over and adjust the heat level. For indirect grilling, place the food over the unlit burner(s), light the burner(s) on the opposite side, and close the lid.

Gas grills tend to produce less intense heat than grills fired with live coals, so they benefit from at least 15 minutes' preheating with the lid closed before you grill. If your grills does not have a built-in thermometer, use an oven thermometer, set at rack level, to check the temperature of your gas grill.

Whether you are grilling with charcoal or with gas, be sure to clean the grill rack with a wire brush after heating and before placing food on it and oil both food and rack to prevent sticking. The easiest way to do this is to pour a little oil onto a wadded-up paper towel and use tongs to rub the rack with it.

Many of the recipes in this book call for grilling delicate or small pieces of food that can easily slip through the rack. For these items you will want to use a basket—either a shaker basket, which holds small pieces, or a fish basket, which allows you to turn fish without fear of losing it. Or, you can line a portion of the grill with heavy-duty aluminium foil and place the food on it. This technique may extend cooking times slightly.

Creating the healthy meal

A commitment to eating a healthy diet based on vegetables, fruits, legumes and whole grains may mean making some lifestyle changes. For example, you may need to modify your shopping habits, visiting the market more often for seasonal fresh produce, or to reduce the portions of meat you eat if you have grown accustomed to large portions. But the rewards will quickly be evident.

To find the best fresh produce, seek out just-harvested, locally grown vegetables and fruits in season at a good produce market or a natural-foods store. Or better yet, make a visit to a farmers' market one of your weekend outings. Although organic produce costs more, pesticide-free vegetables and fruits picked at the peak

of ripeness at local farms also taste better and are more densely packed with nutrients.

The colourful eating philosophy of the New Healthy Kitchen emphasises plant foods, but it doesn't exclude a variety of meats and dairy products. These ingredients add flavour, interest, texture and nutrients to a wide selection of healthy dishes.

Meat, dairy and other animal foods appeal to our bodies' craving for nutrient-rich calories, but it is easy to overindulge in these items, especially when you lead a typically sedentary modern life. The secret is to find balance in enjoying these ingredients. Animal foods contribute important proteins and vitamins to the diet, so they have a place in the New Healthy Kitchen. But they should play a co-starring role alongside grain and vegetables, rather than dominate the dinner plate. Keep your portions modest: a reasonable portion of cooked, boneless meat, poultry or seafood is about the size of a deck of playing cards. Remember, too, that certain meats and many cheeses can act as seasoning elements, rather than main events.

While too much fat adds excessive calories to the diet, a certain amount of fat is essential for the body to function properly. Fat also gives the body the sensation of being satiated, which helps us to avoid overeating. Luckily, grilling is a cooking method that inherently adds little fat. Most of the recipes in this book use olive or rape seed oil as the primary fat for oiling food for grilling. These oils are high in monounsaturated fat, which raises the level of good cholesterol and lowers the bad. Fish and shellfish contribute healthy fats and play a key role in the New Healthy Kitchen.

Herbs and spices are essential flavour boosters in creating healthy dishes. A simple scattering of finely chopped fresh parsley adds not only colour and intense flavour to many different foods, but also valuable green antioxidants. Vinegar, citrus juice and citrus zest are other important flavourings in the New Healthy Kitchen. They contribute an acidic note that heightens other flavours without making a dish taste heavy.

The simple decision to cook your meals at home, rather than load up on take aways or eat in restaurants, is an important step toward healthier eating. The recipes in the New Healthy Kitchen are deliberately easy and streamlined. Preparation and cooking times are listed at the beginning of each recipe to help you fit their assembly into your daily routine. Many dishes can be prepared in half an hour or a little more, making them perfect for a midweek family supper. If you shop and cook more frequently, you will find that both activities become more of a habit, even if you a lead a busy life. And finally, the rewards are great. Eating meals at home is often the highlight of the day. It bonds couples and families together and makes us appreciate all the wonderful foods nature has provided us.

aubergines prunes blackberries

PURPLE AND BLUE FRUITS AND VEGETABLES PROMOTE

purple carrots blackcurrants

MEMORY FUNCTION • HELP PROMOTE URINARY TRACT

lavender blue potatoes purple

HEALTH • BOOST THE IMMUNE SYSTEM • HELP PROMOTE

cabbage raisins black grapes

HEALTHY AGEING • OFFER ANTIOXIDANTS FOR HEALING

purple figs blue plums purple

AND PROTECTION • HELP REDUCE THE RISK OF SOME

peppers purple radishes

CANCERS • PURPLE AND BLUE FRUITS AND VEGETABLES

Purple & blue

The purple and blue harvests, rich in sun-drenched flavour, are good candidates for grilling. Glossy, round plums, plump purple peppers and ripe, juicy blackberries are among the market's showiest items at the end of summer, all of them carrying rich, full flavours and plenty of powerful phytochemicals to keep us feeling young, our hearts pumping and our memories strong.

Grilled aubergine has proven it can be wonderfully versatile. Thin slices can be rolled up with feta cheese for an elegant starter (page 23), or halved and tossed with chicken, tomatoes and olives for a satisfying main course (page 33). Sweet purple figs, with chicken and onions (page 33), or serve endive and fennel as a simple salad (page 27), take on a sweet caramelisation from the heat of the grill.

Juxtaposing the smoky flavours of grilled foods with raw fresh ingredients is one of the best ways to achieve both light and savoury tastes as well as the maximum nutritional value. For example, shavings of raw purple asparagus are an ideal partner to tender grilled salmon (page 30), while seared scallops mix perfectly with a dressing made from purple peppers (page 23).

Grilled purple and blue fruits are showcased for dessert, too, with plums topped with a light cream (page 34) and figs with vanilla-laced ricotta and lemon zest and drizzled with honey (page 29).

SPRING	SUMMER	AUTUMN	WINTER
purple asparagus	purple peppers	purple-tipped Belgian endive	purple-tipped Belgian endive
purple-tipped Belgian endive	blackberries	purple peppers	purple cabbage
blueberries	blueberries	blueberries	purple carrots
purple cabbage	fresh blackcurrants	purple cabbage	currants
purple carrots	aubergine	purple carrots	blue, purple & black grapes
currants	purple figs	dried currants	black olives
blue, purple & black grapes	lavender	aubergine	blue potatoes
prunes	blue, purple & black plums	purple figs	prunes
raisins	purple & black tomatoes	blue, purple & black grapes	raisins
purple radishes		blue, purple & black plums	
		blue potatoes	
		prunes	
		raisins	

grilled aubergine & feta cheese rolls

2 medium aubergines, about 750 g (1½ lb) total

2 Tbsp extra-virgin olive oil, plus extra as needed

250 g (8 oz) feta cheese, crumbled

Zest of 1 lemon, plus lemon juice for drizzling

2 Tbsp chopped fresh parsley

1 tsp fresh thyme leaves

Chopped purple pepper and spring onion for garnish

Build a fire in a charcoal grill for cooking over medium heat or preheat a gas grill to 180°C (350°F). Oil grill rack. Cut aubergines lengthways into slices about 6 mm (¼ in) thick. Brush slices on both sides with olive oil and sprinkle with salt and pepper. Grill, turning once, until golden and softened, 4–5 minutes per side. Remove from heat and place in a paper bag or sealed container to steam and cool (this softens them fully and makes them more tender). Leave to cool to room temperature, about 20 minutes.

In a bowl, toss feta with 2 Tbsp olive oil, lemon zest, parsley and thyme. Place about 2 Tbsp of feta mixture along short edge of a grilled aubergine slice and roll up tightly to enclose. Repeat to make remaining rolls.

Arrange rolls, seam side down, on a serving platter or individual plates. Drizzle with olive oil and lemon juice and serve at room temperature, garnished with pepper and spring onion.

To cook: 10 minutes, plus 20 minutes to cool

To prepare: 10 minutes

6 starter servings (12–14 rolls)

scallops with pepper dressing

16 fresh sea scallops

3 Tbsp extra-virgin olive oil

1½ tsp ground cumin

¼ tsp red pepper flakes

Zest and juice of 1 lime

Sugar

1 large purple pepper, seeded and very finely diced

1 spring onion, including tender green part, thinly sliced

1 small clove garlic, crushed

2 tsp white wine vinegar

Put scallops in a bowl. Add 2 Tbsp olive oil, 1 tsp cumin, red pepper flakes, lime zest, a pinch of sugar and salt and black pepper to taste. Turn to coat evenly. Cover and refrigerate for 30 minutes–6 hours.

In another bowl, stir together pepper, spring onion, garlic, remaining 1 Tbsp olive oil, vinegar, remaining ½ tsp cumin and a pinch of sugar to make a dressing. Taste and adjust seasoning. Leave to stand for 30 minutes to combine flavours.

Build a fire in a charcoal grill for cooking over high heat or preheat a gas grill to 200°C (400°F). Oil grill rack. Grill scallops for about 1 minute per side, just to sear. They should be slightly translucent in the center; do not overcook or they will be rubbery.

Divide dressing among 4 warmed plates. Top each serving with 4 scallops. Drizzle with lime juice and serve at once.

To prepare: 10 minutes, plus 30 minutes to marinate

To cook: 2 minutes

4 servings

grilled pizzas with blue potatoes & onions

Pizza Dough

410 ml (13 fl oz) warm water (about 40°C/ 105°F)

1 pack 15 g (½ oz) active dry yeast

1 tsp sugar

1 tsp salt

2 Tbsp olive oil

About 625 g (1 lb 4 oz) plain flour

Caramelised Onions

2 Tbsp olive oil

3 large red onions, halved and each half thinly sliced

1 Tbsp dark brown sugar

1 Tbsp balsamic vinegar

1 tsp fresh rosemary leaves, chopped

500 g (1 lb) blue potatoes, steamed until tender and sliced

250 g (8 oz) mozzarella cheese, shredded

185 g (6 oz) fresh goat's cheese or feta cheese, crumbled

40 g (1¼ oz) pine nuts, toasted (page 27)

Finely chopped fresh rosemary for garnish

For Dough: Put warm water in a small bowl and stir in yeast and sugar. Leave to stand until foamy, about 5 minutes. Transfer to a food processor and add salt, olive oil and 470 g (15 oz) flour. Process until a ball forms, 2–3 minutes. If dough is too sticky add a little more flour. Dough should be slightly sticky and soft. Alternatively, mix in a stand mixer or in a bowl with a wooden spoon. Place dough on a lightly floured work surface and knead until smooth and elastic, about 7 minutes. Put dough in an oiled bowl, turn to coat, and cover with a damp towel. Leave to rise in a warm place until doubled in bulk, 1½–2 hours.

For Onions: Heat olive oil in a large sauté pan over medium heat. Add onions, brown sugar, vinegar, rosemary, 125 ml (4 fl oz) water, ½ tsp salt and several grindings of pepper and stir to mix. Cover and cook until onions are soft, about 15 minutes. Uncover and cook until all liquid has evaporated and onions are golden, 3–5 minutes more. Remove from heat.

Build a fire in a charcoal grill for cooking over medium-high heat or preheat a gas grill to 190°C (375°F). Line a baking sheet with a double layer of heavy-duty aluminium foil and sprinkle lightly with flour. For easy assembly, arrange onions, potatoes, mozzarella and goat's cheese and pine nuts on a platter. Punch dough down and divide into 12 balls. Roll out each into a thin round 6 inches (15 cm) in diameter. Place 3 or 4 dough rounds on prepared pan. Slide foil onto grill and cook, uncovered, until bottoms of crusts are lightly golden, about 2 minutes.

Turn crusts and sprinkle with mozzarella. Add a layer of potato slices, then caramelised onions, and then goat's cheese, dividing evenly. Sprinkle with pine nuts and season with salt and pepper. Cover grill and cook until crust is crisp and cooked through and edges are golden and mozzarella is melted, 2–3 minutes more. Repeat to cook other pizzas. As pizzas are cooked, sprinkle with rosemary, cut into wedges, and serve at once.

Notes: If you prefer pizza topping to be crusty and browned, slide grilled pizzas under a preheated grill for a couple of minutes. Store caramelised onions in covered container in refrigerator for up to 3 weeks. Pizza dough freezes well for up to 3 months.

To prepare: 45 minutes, plus 2 hours for dough to rise

To cook: 35 minutes

12 starter servings (twelve 6-inch/15-cm pizzas)

fig & purple endive salad

2 Tbsp currants

2 Tbsp orange juice

4 Tbsp extra-virgin olive oil

1 Tbsp balsamic vinegar

1 tsp sugar

1 tsp Dijon mustard

6 ripe but firm purple figs, halved

2 large heads purple-tipped Belgian endive, cores intact, cut into 2.5-cm (1-in) wedges

1 fennel bulb (about 250 g/8 oz) trimmed and thinly sliced lengthways

1 Tbsp lemon juice

2 Tbsp pine nuts, toasted (see Note)

Build a fire in a charcoal grill for cooking over medium heat or preheat a gas grill to 180°C (350°F). Oil grill rack.

Combine currants and orange juice in a microwave-safe bowl, cover and microwave on high for 1 minute. In a large bowl, whisk together 3 Tbsp olive oil, vinegar, sugar, mustard, ½ tsp salt and a few grindings of pepper. Stir in currant mixture. Leave dressing to stand for 15 minutes.

In a bowl, combine figs, endive, fennel, remaining 1 Tbsp olive oil and lemon juice and toss to coat evenly. Grill, turning often, until vegetables are wilted and figs are softened, about 5 minutes. Remove to bowl with dressing and toss gently to mix. Taste and adjust seasoning. Arrange on a serving platter and serve at once, garnished with pine nuts.

Note: To toast pine nuts, put them in a small, dry frying pan over medium heat. Stir often until just starting to turn golden, about 2 minutes; watch carefully or they may burn. Remove at once to a plate to cool.

To prepare: 10 minutes, plus 15 minutes to stand

To cook: 7 minutes

4–6 side-dish servings

halibut & purple grapes

750 g (1½ lb) skinless halibut or other firm white fish fillets, cut into 4-cm (1½-in) pieces

Zest of 1 lime

16 large seedless purple grapes

60 ml (2 fl oz) orange juice

2 Tbsp lime juice

4 tsp chopped fresh dill

2 tsp butter

Build a fire in a charcoal grill for cooking over medium heat or preheat a gas grill to 180°C (350°F).

Put fish in a bowl. Add lime zest, ¾ tsp salt and several grindings of pepper. Turn fish to coat evenly. Cut out four 30-cm (12-in) squares of heavy-duty aluminium foil. Arrange squares on a work surface and divide fish and grapes evenly among them, mounding in centres. Stir orange and lime juices together in a bowl and spoon 1½ Tbsp over each portion. Sprinkle each with 1 tsp dill and dot with ½ tsp butter. Fold foil over fish and crimp edges to seal.

Arrange parcels on grill and cook for 7 minutes. Remove one parcel, open carefully, and test for doneness; fish should just flake in centre when prodded with a fork and should be opaque throughout. If not done, reseal, return to grill and cook all parcels 1–3 minutes more. Open the parcels and arrange the contents on warmed serving plates, or let diners open their own parcels at the table.

Note: Serve with couscous, brown rice or boiled new potatoes and a simple green salad.

To prepare: 10 minutes

To cook: 10 minutes

4 servings

bacon-wrapped prunes

Wrap pitted prunes in bacon, securing the bacon with cocktail sticks. Grill wrapped prunes over medium-high heat, turning them often, until the bacon is crisp. Prunes get very hot on the grill, so leave to cool a little before serving.

grilled blue potatoes

Dice blue potatoes and mound on squares of heavy-duty foil. Season with olive oil, chopped garlic, fresh rosemary and thyme, lemon juice, salt and pepper. Close into pouches and grill over medium heat until tender, about 15 minutes.

grilled purple cabbage

Thinly slice a head of purple cabbage and
toss with grape seed oil, grated ginger,
salt and pepper. Put in an oiled basket
and grill over medium-high heat, shaking
often, until wilted. Garnish with rice
vinegar, sesame oil and sesame seeds.

figs with ricotta

Halve purple figs and brush cut sides
with rape seed oil. Grill over medium-
high heat until softened and lightly
browned. Place atop small scoops of
ricotta cheese mixed with a little lemon
zest and vanilla extract and drizzle
with honey.

grilled salmon with purple asparagus slaw

750 g (1½ lb) skinless salmon fillets, cut on diagonal into slices 12 mm (½ in) thick

2 Tbsp finely chopped fresh coriander

4 tsp olive oil

2 tsp soy sauce

Zest of 1 lime

Dressing

60 ml (2 fl oz) lime juice

1 Tbsp grape seed or rape seed oil

2 tsp Asian sesame oil

1 tsp soy sauce

1 tsp grated fresh ginger

½ tsp sugar

Purple Asparagus Slaw

500 g (1 lb) purple asparagus, tough ends snapped off

2 oranges, peeled, segmented and diced

2 spring onions, including tender green parts, thinly sliced

2 Tbsp chopped fresh coriander

2 Tbsp sesame seeds, toasted (page 45)

Put fish in a bowl. Add coriander, olive oil, soy sauce and lime zest. Turn fish to coat evenly. Cover and refrigerate for 30 minutes–6 hours. Remove from the refrigerator 15 minutes before grilling.

For Dressing: In a glass measuring jug or a jar with a tight-fitting lid, combine lime juice, grape seed and sesame oils, soy sauce, ginger, sugar, ½ tsp salt and several grindings of pepper. Whisk or cover and shake to combine thoroughly. Taste and adjust seasoning.

For Asparagus Slaw: Using a mandoline, a vegetable peeler, or the large holes on a box grater-shredder, shred asparagus, discarding any woody or tough pieces. Place in a bowl. Add oranges, spring onions, coriander and sesame seeds. Pour dressing over and toss to mix well. Cover and refrigerate until ready to serve, up to 4 hours.

Build a fire in a charcoal grill for cooking over medium heat. If using a gas grill, preheat to high heat (200°C/400°F) and then reduce heat to medium (180°C/350°F) for cooking.

Arrange salmon in a single layer in an oiled grill basket or on oiled heavy-duty foil. Sprinkle the fillets with a little pepper. Place basket on or slide foil onto grill. Cover and cook, turning once, until fish just flakes when prodded in thickest part with a fork but is still slightly translucent in the very centre, about 3 minutes per side. Remove to a platter, tent with foil, and leave to rest for 3–4 minutes.

Divide asparagus slaw among warmed serving plates and top with salmon. Serve at once.

To prepare: 20 minutes, plus 30 minutes to marinate

To cook: 10 minutes

4 servings

chicken, aubergine & tomato salad

80 ml (3 fl oz) olive oil

80 ml (3 fl oz) lemon juice

3 Tbsp homemade or purchased basil pesto

Zest of 1 lemon

4 skinless, boneless chicken breasts, sliced on diagonal

1 aubergine

375 g (12 oz) black or red cherry tomatoes, halved

155 g (5 oz) stoned Kalamata or other rich-flavoured black olives

280 g (9 oz) mixed tender salad greens

In a glass measuring jug, stir together olive oil, lemon juice, pesto and lemon zest. Pour two-thirds of mixture into a bowl to use as a marinade; set aside remainder for dressing. Add sliced chicken to bowl and coat with marinade. Cover and refrigerate for 30 minutes–6 hours.

Build a fire in a charcoal grill for cooking over medium heat or preheat a gas grill to 180°C (350°F). Oil grill rack. Halve aubergine lengthways, then cut each half crossways into slices 12 mm (½ in) thick. Brush aubergine slices on both sides with olive oil and sprinkle with salt and pepper. Remove chicken from marinade, discarding marinade. Arrange chicken and aubergine on hot grill. Grill, turning once, until aubergine is golden and chicken is opaque throughout, 3–4 minutes per side. Remove to a serving bowl and leave to cool completely.

Add reserved pesto mixture, tomatoes, olives and salad greens. Toss gently to combine. Serve at room temperature.

To prepare: 10 minutes, plus 30 minutes to marinate

To cook: 10 minutes

4 servings

chicken & fig kebabs

1 Tbsp olive oil

1 Tbsp balsamic vinegar

2 tsp maple syrup

¼ tsp Chinese five-spice powder

750 g (1½ lb) skinless, boneless chicken thighs or breasts, cut into 5-cm (2-in) cubes

16 boiling onions

4 large fresh purple figs, quartered

In a bowl, combine olive oil, vinegar, maple syrup and five-spice powder. Add chicken and turn to coat. Cover and refrigerate for 30 minutes–4 hours. Remove from refrigerator 15–20 minutes before grilling.

Soak 8 wooden skewers in water to cover for 30 minutes. Build a fire in a charcoal grill for cooking over medium heat or preheat a gas grill to 180°C (350°F). Oil grill rack.

Bring a saucepan of water to the boil. Add onions, return to the boil, and cook for 2 minutes. Drain in a colander and place under cold running water until cool to the touch. Trim off stem and root ends and gently slip off skins, keeping onions intact.

Thread chicken, onions and figs onto skewers. Grill kebabs, turning often, until chicken is opaque throughout, 10–12 minutes. Allow 2 kebabs per serving, or remove chicken, figs and onions from skewers and arrange on a warmed serving platter.

To prepare: 15 minutes, plus 30 minutes to marinate

To cook: 12 minutes

4 servings

grilled plums
with kirsch cream

9 large black plums, halved
and stoned

2 Tbsp caster sugar

2 Tbsp kirsch

Rape seed or grape seed oil

2 tsp butter, cut into 18 tiny bits

250 ml (8 fl oz) double cream

1 Tbsp icing sugar

1 tsp vanilla extract

Place plums cut side up in a shallow dish. Sprinkle with caster sugar and drizzle with 1 Tbsp kirsch. Leave to stand for 30 minutes–4 hours.

Build a fire in a charcoal grill for cooking over medium heat or preheat a gas grill to 180°C (350°F). Oil grill rack. Arrange plums, cut side down, on grill. Cook until cut sides are lightly browned and caramelised, about 2 minutes. Turn plum halves over and put a bit of butter into each cavity. Cook until partially tender, 2–3 minutes more. Remove from heat and leave to cool slightly.

In a deep bowl, beat cream until soft peaks form. Using a rubber spatula, fold in icing sugar, vanilla and remaining 1 Tbsp kirsch.

Arrange 3 plum halves on each dessert plate. Dollop with kirsch cream and serve at once.

Note: Cover and refrigerate grilled plums for up to 12 hours. Bring to room temperature before serving. Whip cream just before serving.

*To prepare: 10 minutes,
plus 30 minutes to stand*

To cook: 5 minutes

6 dessert servings

grilled berry parcels

500 g (1 lb) fresh or
frozen blackberries

250 g (8 oz) fresh or
frozen blueberries

2 just-ripe large bananas, peeled
and thickly sliced on diagonal

1 tsp vanilla extract

90 g (3 oz) sugar

1 Tbsp cornflour

Build a fire in a charcoal grill for cooking over medium heat or preheat a gas grill to 180°C (350°F).

In a large bowl, combine berries, bananas and vanilla and stir to combine. In another bowl, stir together sugar and cornflour.

Cut out six 30-cm (12-in) squares of heavy-duty aluminium foil. Arrange squares on a work surface and divide fruit mixture evenly among them, mounding in centres. Sprinkle with sugar mixture.
Fold foil over fruit and crimp edges to seal.

Arrange parcels on grill and cook until fruit has softened, about 10 minutes. Remove parcels to dessert plates and serve at once.

Note: You can empty the contents of the parcels onto plates before serving, or diners can savour the fragrant aromas of the berries when they open their own parcels at the table.

To prepare: 5 minutes

To cook: 10 minutes

6 dessert servings

avocados cucumbers spinach

GREEN FRUITS AND VEGETABLES BOOST THE IMMUNE

watercress rocket asparagus

SYSTEM • PROMOTE EYE HEALTH • HELP BUILD STRONG

mint broccoli snow peas leeks

BONES • BUILD STRONG TEETH • OFFER ANTIOXIDANTS

lettuce courgettes green chillis

FOR HEALING AND PROTECTION • REDUCE THE RISK OF

endive brussels sprouts limes

CERTAIN CANCERS • GREEN FRUITS AND VEGETABLES

green tea kiwifruits artichokes

BOOST THE IMMUNE SYSTEM • PROMOTE EYE HEALTH

Green

Grilled green vegetables and fruits are bright, cool and refreshing in the heat of summer, and deeply coloured, warm and fortifying in the cooler months of the year. Their varied flavours, sizes, and shapes—small, flowerlike artichokes; round, tart apples; long, thin green beans—make it easy to create simple grilled meals that are always different and enticing.

In spring and summer, purée peppery green rocket with sprightly mint for a pesto to accompany tender grilled lamb chops (page 51). As the weather cools, top bright green broccoli gratin with a mix of capers, bread crumbs, and Parmesan and grill until golden (page 51), or whisk together an old-fashioned pancake batter, fold in some green apple slices, and cook the pancakes on the grill on a lazy weekend morning (page 52).

You can also add interest to grilled green vegetables by following the traditions of kitchens around the world. For example, grill green Belgian endive as French cooks do, and then top with blue cheese and walnuts (page 41). You might also make grilled fish tacos and accompany them with a green cabbage salad in the style of Mexico (page 42), or coat chicken with a spice-scented yoghurt marinade that recalls the flavours of India (page 48). In each case, you are delivering both great flavours and a nutrient-rich dietary regimen.

SPRING	SUMMER	AUTUMN	WINTER
artichokes	rocket	green apples	green apples
asparagus	avocados (Hass)	artichokes	avocados (Fuerte)
green peppers	green chillis	bok choy	bok choy
endive	cucumbers	broccoli	broccoli
fava beans	green figs	sprouting broccoli	sprouting broccoli
green beans	green beans	Brussels sprouts	Brussels sprouts
kiwifruits	spring onions	green cabbage	green cabbage
limes	herbs	endive	celery
lettuce	limes	green grapes	endive
green pears	green-fleshed melons	kale	kale
mangetout peas	okra	green pears	kiwifruits
sugar snap peas	sugar snap peas	spinach	snow peas
spinach	spinach	Swiss chard	spinach
watercress	courgettes	watercress	watercress

belgian endive with blue cheese & walnuts

90 g (3 oz) walnut pieces

4 heads Belgian endive, cores intact, cut lengthways into 6 wedges

2 Tbsp olive oil

2 Tbsp lemon juice

125 g (4 oz) blue cheese, crumbled

Place walnuts in a dry frying pan over medium heat. Stir until golden and toasted, 3–4 minutes. Remove at once to a plate. Set aside.

Put endives in a shallow dish. Stir olive oil, lemon juice, ½ tsp salt and several grindings of black pepper together in a small bowl. Pour over endives and turn to coat evenly. Leave to marinate at room temperature for 30 minutes, or cover and refrigerate for up to 4 hours.

Preheat grill. Arrange endives on a baking sheet cut side up. Slide under grill 10 cm (4 in) from heat source and grill, turning once, until softened and starting to caramelise, about 2 minutes per side. Remove to a serving platter and scatter blue cheese and walnuts on top. Serve at once.

Note: This dish makes a nice starter and is also good as a side dish with grilled chicken or pork. Instead of grilling, you can cook the endives over medium-high heat for 2 minutes per side.

To prepare: 10 minutes, plus 30 minutes to marinate

To cook: 5 minutes

4 starter or side-dish servings

spring onions with anchovy sauce

1 tin (50 g / 2 oz) olive oil-packed anchovy fillets, with oil

2 cloves garlic, crushed

2 stoned green olives

1 Tbsp red wine vinegar

2 Tbsp extra-virgin olive oil

16–20 spring onions, trimmed of root ends and top thirds

Combine anchovies and their oil, garlic, olives, vinegar and olive oil in a food processor or blender and process until smooth. Or combine ingredients except for olive oil in a mortar and pound with a pestle until evenly mashed, then gradually stir in oil until smooth. Season with several grindings of pepper. Transfer sauce to a small serving bowl. Cover and refrigerate for 2 hours to combine flavours.

Build a fire in a charcoal grill for cooking over medium heat or preheat a gas grill to 180°C (350°F). Oil grill rack. Grill onions, placing them perpendicular to rack and turning often, until softened and lightly browned, about 7 minutes. Pile onions onto a serving plate and serve. Pass sauce at table.

Note: This rich sauce has a spoonable consistency. For a milder dipping sauce, thin with additional olive oil. Store sauce in a covered container in refrigerator for up to 1 week.

To prepare: 10 minutes, plus 2 hours to marinate

To cook: 7 minutes

4 side-dish servings

grilled fish tacos with green cabbage salad

500 g (1 lb) skinless halibut or other firm white fish fillets, cut into strips about 7.5 cm (3 in) long and 2.5 cm (1 in) wide

2 tsp Cajun spice mix

2 tsp olive oil

375 g (12 oz) finely shredded green cabbage

1 tsp sugar

1 small green chilli, seeded and finely chopped

2 spring onions, including tender green parts, finely chopped

2 Tbsp finely chopped fresh coriander

4 Tbsp lime juice

2 avocados, stoned and peeled

8–10 fresh corn or small flour tortillas, warmed

Put fish in a bowl. Sprinkle with spice mix, olive oil and ½ tsp salt and turn fish to coat evenly. Cover and refrigerate for 30 minutes–4 hours. Remove from the refrigerator 15 minutes before grilling.

Build a fire in a charcoal grill for cooking over medium heat. If using a gas grill, preheat to high heat (200°C/400°F) and then reduce heat to medium (180°C/350°F) for cooking.

In a bowl, combine cabbage, sugar and ½ tsp salt. Work cabbage between your fingers to soften and moisten. Add chilli, spring onions, coriander, 2 Tbsp lime juice and several grindings of pepper and toss to mix well. Taste and adjust seasoning. Set aside at room temperature to allow flavours to blend.

Mash avocados in a small bowl and stir in remaining 2 Tbsp lime juice. Cover and refrigerate until ready to serve.

Arrange fish in a single layer in an oiled grill basket or on oiled heavy-duty aluminium foil. Place basket on or slide foil onto grill. Grill, turning once, until fish just starts to flake when prodded with a fork and is opaque throughout, about 2 minutes per side. Divide cabbage salad among tortillas and top with fish and a dollop of avocado. Serve at once.

To prepare: 15 minutes, plus 30 minutes to marinate

To cook: 4 minutes

4 servings

trout & green pear salad

4 skinless trout or salmon fillets, each about 155 g (5 oz) and 2.5 cm (1 in) thick

2 Tbsp finely chopped fresh chervil or parsley

Olive oil

2 just-ripe crisp green pears, halved, cored and cut into thin wedges (10–12 wedges per pear)

2 Tbsp lime juice

1 Tbsp lemon juice

1 bunch watercress, stemmed

2 Tbsp flaked almonds (see Note), toasted

Build a fire in a charcoal grill for cooking over medium-high heat or preheat gas grill to 190°C (375°F). Sprinkle fillets with chervil and season with salt and pepper. Brush with a little oil.

Combine pears with lime and lemon juices in a mixing bowl and toss to coat. Set aside. Arrange fish in a single layer in an oiled grill basket or on oiled heavy-duty aluminium foil. Place basket or slide foil onto grill. Cover grill and cook, turning once, until flesh just flakes when prodded with a fork and is barely opaque in centre, about 3 minutes per side. Remove to a plate, tent with foil, and leave to rest for 5 minutes.

Add watercress to pears and toss gently to combine. Break trout into salad in bite-sized chunks. Add almonds, season to taste with salt and pepper and toss again gently. Divide among individual plates and serve.

Note: Toast flaked almonds or small seeds in a small, dry frying pan over medium heat. Toast, stirring often, until just starting to turn golden, about 2 minutes; watch closely, as they burn easily. Remove at once to a plate.

To prepare: 15 minutes

To cook: 6 minutes

4 servings

grilled halibut with limes

3 limes

4 halibut or other firm white fish fillets, about 185 g (6 oz) each

1 Tbsp olive oil

1 tsp sugar

1 tsp whole-grain mustard

125 g (4 oz) watercress, tough stems removed

Grate zest from 1 lime and set aside. Reserve zested lime for another use. Arrange fillets in a single layer in a shallow dish. Whisk olive oil, sugar, mustard and zest together in a small bowl. Brush fish on both sides with zest mixture. Cover and refrigerate for 30 minutes–1 hour.

Build a fire in charcoal grill for cooking over medium heat or preheat gas grill to 180°C (350°F). Arrange fish in an oiled grill basket or on oiled heavy-duty aluminium foil and season lightly with salt and pepper. Place basket or slide foil onto grill. Cover grill and cook, turning once, until flesh just flakes in thickest part when prodded with a fork and is still translucent only in the centre, about 4 minutes per side. Remove to a plate, tent with foil, and stand for 5 minutes. Meanwhile, cut remaining 2 limes in half and place on grill, cut side down. Heat until lightly grill-marked, about 3 minutes.

Make a bed of watercress on each warmed plate and arrange fish on top. Serve at once, garnished with grilled lime halves. Diners can squeeze the lime juice or slice off the peel and eat the grilled fruit.

To prepare: 5 minutes, plus 30 minutes to marinate

To cook: 12 minutes

4 servings

crisp green apple & celery salad

Cut 2 cored, unpeeled green apples into matchsticks and toss with lemon juice, walnut oil, thinly sliced celery and spring onions, salt, pepper and toasted coriander seeds. Serve with grilled seafood or chicken.

grilled artichoke salad

Oil-packed artichoke hearts provide an easy alternative to trimming fresh ones for the grill. Drain and cut in half lengthwise. Grill over medium heat until lightly browned on all sides. Toss with a garlicky vinaigrette and chopped herbs.

honeydew prosciutto wraps

Wrap chunks of honeydew melon or green figs in prosciutto. Brush lightly with olive oil and grill over high heat until fruit is warm and prosciutto is lightly browned. Serve as a starter on a bed of rocket leaves.

grilled broad beans

Grill broad beans in the pods over medium-high heat until pods are blackened and soft. Cool, then shell beans and peel each one. Toss with olive oil, salt and pepper. Top with toasted hazelnuts and pecorino shavings.

chicken, avocado & spinach salad

1 Tbsp cumin seeds

1 tsp fennel seeds

250 g (8 oz) plain low-fat yoghurt

4 Tbsp olive oil

3 cloves garlic, crushed

2 tsp paprika

4 skinless, boneless chicken breasts

155 g (5 oz) baby spinach leaves

2 avocados, stoned, peeled and cut into thin wedges

1 grilled red pepper (page 120), peeled, seeded and thinly sliced (optional)

30 g (1 oz) flaked almonds, toasted (page 45)

Juice of 1 lemon

Put cumin and fennel seeds in a small, dry frying pan over medium heat and toast, stirring often, until fragrant, about 1 minute; watch closely as they burn easily. Grind coarsely with a mortar and pestle or spice grinder. Combine ground seeds, yoghurt, 2 Tbsp olive oil, garlic, paprika and ½ tsp salt in a large bowl and stir to mix well. Reserve one-third of mixture for dressing before serving. Add chicken to bowl and stir to coat evenly. Cover and refrigerate for 30 minutes–12 hours.

Preheat grill. Cut chicken into long, thick slices (4 or 5 per breast). Spread slices in a single layer on a baking sheet lined with foil. Sprinkle with salt and pepper and brush with oil. Slide under grill about 10 cm (4 in) from heat source and grill, turning once, until browned and opaque throughout, 10–12 minutes. Remove to a large bowl and rest for 5 minutes. Add reserved yogurt mixture, stir to coat evenly, and let cool for 5–10 minutes more.

Add spinach, avocados, grilled pepper (if using) and almonds to bowl. Drizzle with remaining 2 Tbsp olive oil and lemon juice and toss gently to combine. To serve, pile onto a platter or salad plates. Drizzle any dressing remaining in bowl over salads and serve.

To prepare: 10 minutes, plus 30 minutes to marinate

To cook: 15 minutes, plus 15 minutes to cool

4 servings

green & yellow beans with almonds

500 g (1 lb) mixed green and yellow wax beans, ends trimmed

1½ Tbsp plus 1 tsp extra-virgin olive oil

Zest of 1 lemon

75 g (2½ oz) roasted smoked almonds, coarsely chopped

Build a fire in a charcoal grill for cooking over medium heat or preheat gas grill to 180°C (350°F). Bring 500 ml (16 fl oz) water to a boil in a saucepan over high heat. Add 1 tsp salt and beans and boil for 3 minutes. Drain in a colander and place under cold running water to cool. Drain again thoroughly. Toss with 1 tsp olive oil, ½ tsp salt, and several grindings of pepper.

Arrange beans in a single layer in an oiled grill basket. Grill, shaking often, until lightly browned and tender-crisp, 3–4 minutes. Remove to a platter. Stir zest and remaining 1½ Tbsp olive oil together in a small bowl and drizzle over beans. Scatter almonds on top and serve at once.

To prepare: 10 minutes

To cook: 8 minutes

4 side-dish servings

lamb chops with rocket pesto

8 lamb loin or rib chops, trimmed of excess fat

2 Tbsp lemon juice

1 Tbsp olive oil

2 or 3 sprigs mint, lightly bruised

2 cloves garlic, crushed

Rocket Pesto

155 g (5 oz) packed rocket leaves

15 g (½ oz) packed fresh mint leaves

125 ml (4 fl oz) extra-virgin olive oil

1 clove garlic

Zest of 1 lemon

Put lamb chops in a bowl and sprinkle with lemon juice, olive oil, mint, garlic and salt and pepper to taste. Toss to coat evenly. Cover and marinate at room temperature for 30 minutes, or in the refrigerator for up to 4 hours. Bring to room temperature before grilling.

Build a fire in a charcoal grill for cooking over medium-high heat or preheat a gas grill to 190°C (375°F). Oil grill rack.

For Pesto: In a food processor or blender, combine rocket, mint, olive oil, garlic, lemon zest, ½ tsp salt and several grindings of pepper. Process until smooth. Taste and adjust seasoning. Spoon into a small serving bowl and refrigerate until ready to serve.

Grill lamb chops, turning once, until nicely browned and done to your liking, about 3 minutes per side for medium-rare (a meat thermometer inserted in thickest part, away from bone, should read 54°C/130°F). Remove to a serving platter, tent with foil, and rest for 5 minutes. Arrange 2 chops on each warmed plate and serve with pesto.

To prepare: 10 minutes, plus 30 minutes to marinate

To cook: 6 minutes

4 servings

broccoli gratin

2–4 slices country-style bread

4 Tbsp olive oil

60 g (2 oz) grated Parmesan cheese

2 Tbsp capers, drained and finely chopped

2 cloves garlic, crushed

750 g (1½ lb) broccoli, stalks peeled and chopped, heads cut into small florets

3 Tbsp low-fat sour cream

Preheat grill. Remove crusts from bread slices and toast about 10 cm (4 in) from heat source until golden on both sides, about 2 minutes total. Break into large pieces and place in a food processor. Process just to form coarse crumbs, pulsing briefly as they near desired consistency; you don't want fine crumbs for this dish. Measure 185 g (6 oz) crumbs. In a bowl, toss breadcrumbs with olive oil, Parmesan, capers and garlic until evenly combined.

Bring a saucepan three-quarters full of lightly salted water to the boil. Add broccoli and cook for 2 minutes. Drain in a colander and place under cold running water to cool. Drain again thoroughly and arrange in a shallow baking or gratin dish. Spread sour cream over broccoli and sprinkle with breadcrumb mixture. Slide under grill about 15 cm (6 in) from heat source and cook until gratin is heated through and breadcrumbs are golden and crisp, 4–5 minutes. Serve at once.

To prepare: 15 minutes

To cook: 7 minutes

4 side-dish servings

grilled apple pancakes

125 g (4 oz)
soft-wheat flour

250 ml (8 fl oz) skimmed or
whole milk

1 large egg

60 g (2 oz) sugar

1½ tsp baking powder

1 tsp vanilla extract

¼ tsp bicarbonate of soda

¼ tsp ground cloves

¼ tsp salt

2 Tbsp butter, melted

2 green apples, unpeeled

Rape seed oil as needed

Warmed maple syrup for serving
or 2 Tbsp caster sugar mixed with ½
tsp ground cinnamon

Build a fire in a charcoal grill for cooking over medium heat or preheat a gas grill to 180°C (350°F).

In a bowl, combine flour, milk, egg, sugar, baking powder, vanilla, bicarbonate of soda, cloves and salt. Beat with an electric mixer or whisk until smooth. Add melted butter and beat until fully incorporated.

Cut apples into quarters, cut out cores, and slice very thinly. Stir into batter until evenly distributed.

Place a griddle or cast-iron frying pan on grill to preheat. Lightly oil pan and ladle on 2-Tbsp portions of batter, 5 cm (2 in) apart; be sure not to crowd pan. Cover grill and cook until bubbles form on surface of pancakes and bottoms are golden, about 2 minutes. Turn with a spatula, re-cover, and cook until second sides are golden, about 2 minutes more. Remove to a plate, cover with foil, and place near grill to keep warm. Repeat to cook remaining pancakes, lightly oiling pan as needed.

Serve at once, drizzled with syrup or sprinkled with cinnamon sugar.

Note: The batter can be prepared up to 3 hours ahead, covered and refrigerated until ready to use.

To prepare: 10 minutes

To cook: 15 minutes

4 or 5 servings (16 hotcakes)

cauliflower shallots mushrooms

WHITE AND TAN FRUITS AND VEGETABLES CONTAIN

dates turnips bananas tan figs

ANTIOXIDANTS FOR HEALING AND PROTECTION • HELP

tan pears parsnips white corn

MAINTAIN A HEALTHY CHOLESTEROL LEVEL • PROMOTE

potatoes jerusalem artichokes

HEART HEALTH • BOOST THE IMMUNE SYSTEM • SLOW

ginger kohlrabi white peaches

CHOLESTEROL ABSORPTION • WHITE AND TAN FRUITS

garlic white nectarines jicama

AND VEGETABLES OFFER ANTIOXIDANTS FOR HEALING

White & tan

Salads and salsas are favourite menu items in the warm months and are a fresh way to enjoy the white and tan produce of the season. In the spirit of summer's slow, lazy days, the recipes—a white aubergine and onion salad, white corn salsa, white nectarine salsa—are kept simple. As the days cool, autumn's parsnips, fennel and leeks take their places over the fire of the grill.

Nothing evokes summer holidays like the aromas that rise from a grill, and the tan and white family of vegetables and fruits is a perfect match for patio cooking. You might grill white corn on the cob with a herb-flecked butter (page 64), or slice off the kernels and combine them in an attractive dish with green chillis and coriander (page 60).

When the weather is hot, no one wants to be indoors chopping and slicing ingredients, so start your summer meal with simply grilled field mushrooms flavoured with lemon and garlic and served on country-style bread (page 59), and try grilled skewered nectarine wedges paired with a quick ginger-pineapple sauce (page 70) for dessert.

For an autumn lunchtime feast, look no further than spicy turkey sandwiches, heaped with grilled sweet onions (page 60). As the weather grows cooler, you can still fire up the grill to enjoy leeks with a sweet-sour mustard dressing (page 59) or crisp parsnip chips drizzled with lemon and honey (page 65).

SPRING	SUMMER	AUTUMN	WINTER
white asparagus	bananas	cauliflower	cauliflower
bananas	white corn	dates	dates
cauliflower	dates	tan figs	garlic
dates	white aubergine	Jerusalem artichokes	ginger
garlic	tan figs	jicama	Jerusalem artichokes
ginger	garlic	kohlrabi	jicama
jicama	ginger	leeks	leeks
mushrooms	mushrooms	mushrooms	dried mushrooms
onions	white nectarines	onions	onions
parsnips	onions	parsnips	parsnips
tan pears	white peaches	tan pears	celeriac
potatoes	tan pears	potatoes	potatoes
shallots	plantains	shallots	shallots
turnips	potatoes	turnips	turnips

mushroom bruschetta

3 Tbsp olive oil, plus more for drizzling

2 Tbsp lemon juice

1 clove garlic, crushed

500 g (1 lb) field mushrooms, brushed clean and stemmed, cut into slices 6 mm (¼ in) thick

8 slices country-style bread, cut on diagonal 12 mm (½ in) thick

30 g (1 oz) crumbled feta cheese

2 Tbsp thinly sliced fresh basil leaves

In a bowl, stir together olive oil, lemon juice, garlic, ½ tsp salt and several grindings of pepper. Add mushroom slices and turn to coat evenly. Stand for 10 minutes–1 hour.

Build a fire in a charcoal grill for cooking over medium-high heat or preheat a gas grill to 190°C (375°F).

Brush bread slices on both sides with olive oil and grill until lightly browned and grill-marked, about 1 minute per side. You may need to press bread into grill to get nice grill marks. Remove to a platter, cover with foil, and place near grill to keep warm.

Arrange mushroom slices in a single layer in an oiled grill basket or on oiled heavy-duty aluminium foil. Place basket or slide foil onto grill. Grill, turning once, until softened and richly browned, about 3 minutes per side. Divide mushrooms among grilled bread slices, drizzle with olive oil and sprinkle with feta and basil. Serve at once.

To prepare: 10 minutes, plus 10 minutes to marinate

To cook: 8 minutes

4 starter servings

mustard-honey leeks

Dressing

60 ml (2 fl oz) extra-virgin olive oil

2 Tbsp white wine vinegar

2 tsp Dijon mustard

1 tsp honey

500 g (1 lb) baby or small leeks, no more than 12mm–2cm (½–¾ in) thick

Build a fire in a charcoal grill for cooking over medium heat or preheat a gas grill to 180°C (350°F). Oil grill rack.

For Dressing: Whisk olive oil, vinegar, mustard, honey, ½ tsp salt and several grindings of pepper together in a bowl. Set aside.

Bring a large sauté pan of lightly salted water to the boil. If using baby leeks, trim tough green parts and root ends. If using slightly larger leeks, remove any tough or bruised outer leaves, trim, then cut down 5–7.5 cm (2–3 in) through the length, without cutting into the white base. Rinse under cold running water thoroughly to remove any grit, spreading leaves gently but keeping bulbs intact. Add leeks to boiling water and simmer to soften slightly, about 5 minutes. Drain thoroughly.

Brush leeks lightly with olive oil and sprinkle with salt and pepper. Grill, turning often, until lightly browned, 10–12 minutes. Remove to a serving platter. Pour dressing over and turn gently to coat thoroughly. Let stand for 30 minutes. Serve at once, or cover and refrigerate for up to 2 days, then bring to room temperature to serve.

To prepare: 15 minutes, plus 30 minutes to stand

To cook: 20 minutes

4 starter or side-dish servings

turkey sandwiches
with sweet onions

2 tsp ground cumin

½ tsp *each* ground smoked paprika, fennel, cardamom, ginger, cinnamon, and pepper

125 ml (4 fl oz) low-fat or regular mayonnaise

2 Tbsp olive oil

2 cloves garlic, crushed

500 g (1 lb) turkey breast meat, thinly sliced 6 mm (¼ in) thick

2 large sweet onions, sliced in rings 12 mm (½ in) thick

4 sandwich rolls, split

Mixed salad greens, tomato slices and avocado slices for garnish

Stir spices together in a small bowl. Combine 1 tsp spice mixture and mayonnaise in a bowl, stir to mix well and refrigerate. In another small bowl, stir together remaining spice mixture, olive oil, garlic and 1 tsp salt. Pour over turkey in a shallow dish and turn to coat evenly. Cover and refrigerate for 30 minutes–4 hours. Remove from the refrigerator 15 minutes before grilling.

Build a fire in a charcoal grill for cooking over medium heat or preheat a gas grill to 180°C (350°F). Oil grill rack. Brush onion slices on both sides with olive oil. Grill until lightly browned, 4 minutes per side. Add turkey to grill and cook until browned, 2 minutes per side. Meanwhile, continue grilling onions, turning often, until golden and just caramelised, 5–7 minutes more. Remove onions and turkey to a platter.

Grill cut sides of rolls until lightly browned and grill-marked, about 1 minute. Divide turkey among bottoms of rolls. Top with grilled onions. Spread tops of rolls with flavoured mayonnaise. Top sandwiches and serve with garnishes.

To prepare: 10 minutes, plus 30 minutes to marinate

To cook: 15 minutes

4 servings

grilled white corn salad

6 ears white corn, husks and silk removed

Dressing

2 Tbsp *each* olive oil and lime juice

2 cloves garlic, finely chopped

1–2 green chillis, seeded and finely chopped

1 tsp firmly packed light brown sugar

1 tsp ground cumin

½ tsp red pepper flakes

15 g (½ oz) fresh coriander leaves

2 spring onions, including tender green parts, thinly sliced

Build a fire in a charcoal grill for cooking over medium heat or preheat a gas grill to 180°C (350°F). Oil grill rack. Fill a bowl with cold water, add 1 tsp salt and stir to dissolve. Add corn and stand for 10 minutes.

For Dressing: In a bowl, combine olive oil, lime juice, garlic, chilli to taste, brown sugar, cumin, red pepper flakes, ½ tsp salt and several grindings of black pepper. Stir to dissolve sugar and mix well. Set aside.

Drain corn thoroughly, pat dry and brush with olive oil. Grill, turning often, until lightly browned and tender, about 15 minutes. Remove to a platter to cool. When cool to the touch, use a sharp, heavy knife to cut kernels from cobs and put in a mixing bowl.

Add coriander and spring onions and toss gently to combine. Add dressing and again toss gently to coat thoroughly. Taste and adjust seasoning. Arrange on a platter and serve at room temperature.

To prepare: 10 minutes, plus 10 minutes to stand

To cook: 15 minutes

4–6 side-dish servings

grilled lobster tails
with white corn salsa

Dressing

2 Tbsp sesame seeds, toasted (page 45)

1 Tbsp rice vinegar

2 tsp grape seed or rape seed oil

2 tsp finely chopped fresh ginger

½ tsp soy sauce

¼ tsp Asian sesame oil

4 ears white corn, husks and silk removed

1 Tbsp butter, softened

1 tsp Asian sesame oil

1 tsp finely chopped fresh ginger

2 spring onions, white part only, 1 thinly sliced and 1 finely chopped

2 fresh lobster tails, 440 g–470 g (14–15 oz) total, cut in half lengthways and deveined

1 large avocado, stoned, peeled and diced

Build a fire in a charcoal grill for cooking over medium heat or preheat a gas grill to 180°C (350°F). Oil grill rack.

For Dressing: Combine sesame seeds, vinegar, grape seed oil, ginger, soy sauce and ¼ tsp sesame oil in a small bowl and stir to mix well. Set dressing aside.

Fill a bowl with cold water, add 1 tsp salt, and stir to dissolve. Add corn and stand for 10 minutes. Meanwhile, stir butter, 1 tsp sesame oil, ginger and the sliced spring onion together in a small bowl and set aside.

Drain corn thoroughly, pat dry and brush with oil. Grill, turning often, until lightly browned and tender-crisp, 12–15 minutes. Remove to a platter and leave to cool.

Place lobster tails, cut side down, on grill and cook over medium heat until lightly browned, 4–5 minutes. Turn lobster tails and spread butter mixture over cut surfaces. Grill until butter melts and flesh is opaque throughout and firm to the touch, 4–6 minutes more.

While lobster is grilling, use a sharp, heavy knife to cut corn kernels from cobs. Put in a mixing bowl. Add the chopped spring onion and toss gently to combine. Add dressing and avocado and again toss gently to coat thoroughly. Taste and adjust seasoning.

Divide corn salsa among warmed plates and arrange a lobster tail half on each plate. Serve at once.

Note: If using frozen lobster tails, allow to thaw completely before cooking. You can also use a whole lobster. Cut in half lengthways, slicing between eyes and splitting the tail vertically. Place shell side up and grill for about 8 minutes. Turn over and spread flesh sides with flavoured butter and grill for 8–10 minutes more.

To prepare: 15 minutes, plus 10 minutes to stand

To cook: 25 minutes

4 servings

grilled white corn with herb butter

Soak husked ears of white corn in lightly salted cold water for 10 minutes. Brush kernels lightly with oil. Grill over medium heat until lightly browned and tender. Spread with butter mixed with finely chopped garlic, herbs, salt and pepper.

grilled shallots

Grill whole unpeeled shallots over very low or indirect heat until collapsed and blackened, about 25 minutes. Cool then peel. Drizzle with a little olive oil and balsamic vinegar. Scatter with toasted pine nuts. Serve with grilled meats.

grilled parsnip crisps with lemon & honey

Rinse, and peel parsnips and slice lengthways into long, thin slices. Toss with olive oil to coat and grill over medium heat, turning often, until lightly browned. Drizzle with a mixture of honey, lemon zest and juice, and chopped fresh

pesto mushrooms

Brush field mushrooms clean and trim stems. Spoon a little pesto over gill sides. Sprinkle with lemon juice, salt and pepper; dot with butter. Grill, gill side up, over medium-low heat until mushrooms are soft and pesto bubbles.

cuban-style pork
& plantains

Marinade

2 Tbsp olive oil

2 Tbsp *each* orange juice and lime juice

1 Tbsp white wine vinegar

2 tsp maple syrup

2 cloves garlic, crushed

1 Tbsp chopped fresh oregano or 1 tsp dried oregano

1 tsp *each* ground cumin and allspice

½ tsp red pepper flakes (optional)

Grated zest of ½ orange

Grated zest of ½ lime

4 bone-in centre-cut rib or loin pork chops, each about 2 cm (¾ in) thick

4 pineapple slices (page 70), 2.5 cm (1 in) thick, each cut into thirds (optional)

2 yellow plantains

For Marinade: In a glass measuring jug, whisk together olive oil, orange and lime juices, vinegar, maple syrup, garlic, oregano, cumin, allspice, red pepper flakes (if using), orange and lime zests, ¾ tsp salt and ½ tsp pepper.

Put pork and pineapple, if using, in a bowl. Add half of marinade; cover and refrigerate remainder until ready to serve. Turn pork and pineapple to coat evenly. Cover and marinate at room temperature for 20 minutes, or refrigerate for up to 2 hours. Bring to room temperature before grilling.

Build a fire in a charcoal grill for cooking over medium-high heat or preheat a gas grill to 190°C (375°F). Oil grill rack.

Meanwhile, cook plantains whole in their skins in a saucepan of boiling water for 5 minutes. Drain and cool for about 10 minutes. When cool enough to handle, peel off the skins and cut the flesh crossways into slices 2 cm (¾ in) thick.

Remove pork chops and pineapple, if using, from marinade and discard marinade. Grill pork until golden on outside and just faintly pink in centre (a meat thermometer inserted in thickest part, away from bone, should read 63°C/145°F), 2–3 minutes per side. Remove to a platter, tent with foil, and let rest for 5 minutes. Brush plantain slices with olive oil on both sides and sprinkle with salt and pepper. Grill plantains and pineapple, if using, turning once, until softened and lightly browned, 2–3 minutes per side.

Arrange pork and fruit on warmed plates, drizzle with reserved marinade, and serve at once.

To prepare: 15 minutes, plus 20 minutes to marinate

To cook: 15 minutes

6 servings

white aubergine & spring onion salad

Tahini Dressing

2 Tbsp extra-virgin olive oil

2 Tbsp lemon juice

1 Tbsp tahini

2 cloves garlic, finely chopped

4 Asian white slender aubergines, about 500 g (1 lb), cut crossways into slices 6 mm (¼ in)

2 spring onions, white parts only, finely chopped

2 Tbsp finely chopped fresh parsley

Build a fire in a charcoal grill for cooking over medium heat or preheat a gas grill to 180°C (350°F). Oil grill rack.

For Dressing: Whisk oil, lemon juice, tahini and garlic together in a bowl. Set aside.

Brush aubergine slices on both sides with oil and sprinkle with salt and pepper. Grill, turning once, until golden and softened, 4–5 minutes per side. Remove from heat and place in a covered bowl to steam and cool (this softens them fully and makes them more tender).

Add spring onions and parsley to bowl with cooled aubergine. Pour dressing over and toss to coat thoroughly. Taste and adjust seasoning. Stand at room temperature for 30 minutes to combine flavours. Serve at once or cover and refrigerate for up to 8 hours and bring to room temperature before serving.

To prepare: 10 minutes, plus 30 minutes to stand

To cook: 10 minutes

4 starter servings

grilled fennel with indian spices

2 medium or 4 smallish fennel bulbs, about 500 g (1 lb)

Boiling water as needed

3 Tbsp olive oil

2 tsp *each* mustard seeds and ground coriander

1¼ tsp ground cumin

½ tsp *each* ground cloves and cardamom

125 g (4 oz) low-fat or whole plain yoghurt

30 g (1 oz) shredded cucumber

1 Tbsp chopped fresh mint

Trim fennel and slice thinly lengthways. Place fennel in a heatproof bowl, pour over boiling water to cover, and stand for 2 minutes to soften slightly. Drain thoroughly, pat dry and return to bowl. Add oil, mustard seeds, coriander, 1 tsp cumin, cloves, cardamom, ½ tsp salt and several grindings of pepper and toss to mix well and coat evenly. (This step can be done up to 4 hours ahead of grilling.)

Stir yoghurt, cucumber, mint and remaining ¼ tsp cumin together in a bowl. Set mixture aside.

Build a fire in a charcoal grill for cooking over medium heat or preheat a gas grill to 180°C (350°F). Oil grill rack. Grill fennel, turning occasionally, until softened and lightly browned, about 3 minutes per side. Serve at once, with flavoured yoghurt.

To prepare: 10 minutes

To cook: 6 minutes

4 side-dish servings

white nectarine kebabs

Ginger Sauce

250 g (8 oz) chopped fresh pineapple (see Note) or drained unsweetened tinned pineapple

2 Tbsp maple syrup

2 tsp finely chopped fresh ginger

6 white nectarines, quartered and stoned

2 tsp maple syrup

1 tsp lemon juice

1 tsp vanilla extract

Build a fire in a charcoal grill for cooking over medium-low heat or preheat a gas grill to 150°C (300°F). Oil grill rack. Soak 8 wooden skewers in water to cover for 30 minutes.

For Sauce: In a blender or food processor, combine pineapple, 2 Tbsp maple syrup and ginger and process until smooth. Set aside.

Place nectarine quarters in a bowl and toss with 2 tsp maple syrup, lemon juice and vanilla. Thread 3 nectarine pieces onto each skewer. Grill, turning often, until nectarines are tender and lightly browned, about 8 minutes.

Serve warm, accompanied with sauce.

Notes: To prepare fresh pineapple, cut off top and bottom, then stand pineapple upright and slice away peel. Trim away eyes by making shallow, V-shaped cuts in a spiral around the pineapple. Slice crossways, and cut out core from slices with a paring knife or small biscuit cutter. Store leftover sauce in refrigerator for up to 3 days.

To prepare: 10 minutes, plus 30 minutes to soak skewers

To cook: 8 minutes

4–6 dessert servings

grapefruit papayas pineapples

YELLOW AND ORANGE FRUITS AND VEGETABLES HELP

peaches yellow corn pumpkins

PROMOTE HEART HEALTH • HELP REDUCE THE RISK OF

persimmons apricots kumquats

CERTAIN CANCERS • PROMOTE EYE HEALTH • CONTAIN

swedes golden beets carrots

ANTIOXIDANTS FOR HEALING AND PROTECTION • BOOST

yellow apples golden kiwifruits

THE IMMUNE SYSTEM • YELLOW AND ORANGE FRUITS

lemons navel oranges mangoes

AND VEGETABLES OFFER ANTIOXIDANTS FOR HEALING

Yellow & orange

Grilled fresh mahimahi with mango salsa (page 84). Succulent duck breasts served on a bed of papaya and lamb's lettuce (page 81). Grilled snapper and mandarin salad (page 84). Grilled salmon with yellow potato, corn and sweet onion salad (page 78). Grilled apricots with sabayon (page 88). These are dishes you would hope to find at your favourite bistro, but now you can enjoy them at home on a weeknight.

All of these surprisingly simple-to-make dishes use orange and yellow vegetables and fruits, whose bold, rich colours and flavours pair particularly well with a wide range of fish and poultry. The sweet, yet subtle caramelising effect of the grill nicely balances the acid tones of certain tropical fruits, such as papaya and mango, providing the home cook with new ways to serve these nutrition-packed foods.

But more common yellow and orange vegetables—sweet potato, potato, squash, pumpkin—also take well to the grill and are featured here with an array of different dressings. Grilled pumpkin slices are served with a pumpkin seed dressing flavoured with chilli, orange, and coriander (page 77), while slices of grilled sweet potato are drizzled with a lovely sesame miso dressing (page 87). Crookneck squash is complemented by the flavours of fennel and feta (page 87). You may like to mix and match the dressings; many members of the orange family share an affinity for the same ingredient pairings.

SPRING	SUMMER	AUTUMN	WINTER
yellow & orange peppers	apricots	yellow apples	yellow apples
carrots	yellow & orange peppers	dried apricots	dried apricots
grapefruit	corn	golden beets	golden beets
golden kiwifruits	mangoes	yellow & orange peppers	carrots
kumquats	orange-fleshed melon	lemons	grapefruit
lemons	nectarines	navel & mandarin oranges	kumquats
mangoes	Valencia oranges	yellow pears	lemons
navel & mandarin oranges	papayas	persimmons	navel & mandarin oranges
papayas	passion fruit	yellow-fleshed potatoes	yellow pears
yellow-fleshed potatoes	peaches	pumpkins	yellow-fleshed potatoes
sweet potatoes	pineapples	swedes	pumpkins
orange-fleshed winter squash	golden raspberries	sweet potatoes	swedes
	yellow summer squash	orange-fleshed winter squash	sweet potatoes
	yellow tomatoes		orange-fleshed winter squash

yellow tomatoes
with mint & pecorino

2 tsp firmly packed light brown sugar

1 tsp curry powder

6 large yellow tomatoes, cored and halved lengthways

45 g (1½ oz) pecorino cheese, coarsely grated

14 mint leaves, finely chopped

2 spring onions, including tender green parts, finely chopped

1 Tbsp extra-virgin olive oil

Preheat grill. Put sugar, curry powder, 1 tsp salt and several grindings of pepper on a saucer and stir to combine. Press cut surfaces of tomatoes into spice mixture and then arrange, coated side up, on a baking sheet lined with foil.

Slide tomatoes under grill 10–15 cm (4–6 in) from heat source and cook until topping bubbles and starts to caramelise, 10 minutes.

Meanwhile, combine pecorino, mint, spring onions and olive oil in a bowl and stir to mix well. Remove tomatoes to a platter. Sprinkle cheese mixture over tomatoes and serve hot.

To prepare: 10 minutes

To cook: 10 minutes

4–6 side-dish servings

grilled pumpkin with
pumpkin seed dressing

30 g (1 oz) hulled pumpkin seeds

125 ml (4 fl oz) orange juice

1 Tbsp grape seed oil

1 small red chilli, seeded and finely chopped

1 small pumpkin, 375–500 g (12–16 oz), peeled, halved, and seeded

2 Tbsp olive oil

2 spring onions, including tender green parts, thinly sliced

2 Tbsp chopped fresh coriander (optional)

Build a fire in a charcoal grill for cooking over medium-low heat or preheat a gas grill to 150°C (300°F). Oil grill rack.

Place pumpkin seeds in a small, dry frying pan over medium heat and toast, stirring occasionally, until golden, 3–4 minutes. In a blender or food processor, combine pumpkin seeds, orange juice, grape seed oil, chilli, ½ tsp salt and several grindings of pepper and process to make a dressing that is almost smooth but retains some texture.

With a heavy knife, cut pumpkin into 7.5-cm (3-in) wedges, then cut each wedge crossways into slices 6 mm (¼ in) thick. Put in a bowl and add olive oil and salt and pepper to taste. Turn to coat pumpkin evenly.

Grill pumpkin, turning often, until lightly browned and nearly fork-tender, 8–10 minutes. Remove to a cutting board and cool slightly. Put in a bowl. Pour dressing over and toss gently to combine, taking care not to break up pumpkin. Remove to a serving platter and sprinkle with spring onions and coriander, if using. Serve warm or at room temperature.

Note: Before peeling pumpkin, microwave it for 1–2 minutes to soften skin. If pumpkin is organic, you do not need to remove the skin.

To prepare: 20 minutes

To cook: 10 minutes

4–6 side-dish servings

grilled salmon, potato & corn salad

4 salmon fillets, skin on, about 155 g (5 oz) each

60 g (2 oz) tightly packed fresh basil leaves

125 ml (4 fl oz) extra-virgin olive oil

4 ears corn, husks and silk removed

½ lemon

250 g (8 oz) yellow potatoes boiled until tender and diced

2 Tbsp finely chopped sweet onion

185 g (6 oz) yellow cherry tomatoes, halved

Put salmon fillets, flesh side up, in a shallow dish. Combine basil, olive oil, 60 ml (2 fl oz) water, ½ tsp salt and several grindings of pepper in a blender or food processor and process until smooth. Set aside half the basil mixture for dressing. Brush other half over flesh sides of salmon. Cover and refrigerate for 30 minutes–6 hours. Remove from the refrigerator 15 minutes before grilling.

Build a fire in a charcoal grill for cooking over medium heat or preheat a gas grill to 180°C (350°F). Oil grill rack.

Fill a large bowl with cold water, add 1 tsp salt and stir to dissolve. Add corn and stand for 10 minutes.

Drain corn thoroughly, pat dry and brush with olive oil. Grill, turning often, until lightly browned and tender-crisp, about 15 minutes. Remove to a platter and leave to cool.

If using a charcoal grill, let coals burn down to medium-low. If using a gas grill, reduce heat to 158°C (300°F). Arrange fish in an oiled grill basket or place on oiled heavy-duty aluminium foil, fish skin side down. Place basket on or slide foil onto grill. Cover grill and cook until white droplets start to appear on surface, about 8 minutes. Turn carefully and grill just until flesh sides are nicely sealed, about 2 minutes more. Remove to a platter, squeeze half lemon over, tent with foil, and leave to stand for 5 minutes.

Use a sharp, heavy knife to cut kernels from cobs and put in a large bowl. Add potatoes, onion, tomatoes and reserved basil mixture. Toss gently to distribute and coat evenly. Remove and discard skin and any stray bones from salmon and flake in large chunks into bowl. Toss again gently, taking care not to break up salmon. Taste and adjust seasoning. Serve at room temperature.

Note: This salad is also excellent prepared with grilled chicken in place of the salmon.

To prepare: 10 minutes, plus 30 minutes to marinate

To cook: 10 minutes

4 servings

grilled duck breast with papaya

125 ml (4 fl oz) orange juice

Zest of 1 lime, plus 3 Tbsp lime juice

2 Tbsp Thai sweet chilli sauce

2 tsp finely chopped fresh ginger

1 tsp fish sauce

¼ tsp Chinese five-spice powder

4 skinless, boneless duck breasts

Olive oil for brushing

125 g (4 oz) lamb's lettuce

1 firm yet ripe papaya, peeled, seeded and cut into thin wedges

2 spring onions, including tender green parts, thinly sliced

In a glass measuring jug, stir together orange juice, lime zest and juice, chilli sauce, ginger, fish sauce, five-spice powder, ½ tsp salt and several grindings of pepper. Pour half of orange juice mixture into a bowl to use as marinade; cover and refrigerate remainder for dressing. Add duck to bowl with marinade and turn to coat evenly. Cover and refrigerate for 30 minutes–6 hours. Bring to room temperature before grilling.

Build a fire in a charcoal grill for cooking over high heat or preheat a gas grill to 200°C (400°F). Oil grill rack.

Remove duck breast halves from marinade, pat dry and brush with olive oil. (Discard marinade.) Grill, turning once, until golden brown, 3–4 minutes per side, depending on size. Cover grill and cook until duck is still slightly pink in the centre and has a little give when pressed in thickest part (a meat thermometer should read 54°C/135°F), 3–4 minutes more. Remove to a cutting board, tent with foil and leave to rest for 5 minutes.

Arrange a bed of lamb's lettuce and papaya on each plate and sprinkle with spring onions. Cut duck on diagonal into slices and put in a bowl. Add reserved orange juice mixture and toss to coat. Taste and adjust the seasoning if needed. Arrange duck on greens and drizzle with dressing collected in bowl. Serve at once.

To prepare: 10 minutes, plus 30 minutes to marinate

To cook: 10 minutes

4 servings

moroccan carrot salad

Shred carrots with a vegetable peeler and mix with olive oil, a pinch of cumin, a splash of rosewater and salt and pepper. Toss with chopped unsalted pistachios and fresh coriander. Serve with grilled lamb or beef.

orange gazpacho

Purée the flesh of 2 grilled and peeled yellow or orange peppers with 500 ml (16 fl oz) *each* chilled tomato juice and beef stock. Season with salt, pepper and sherry vinegar to taste. Chill and serve.

grilled pineapple

In a shallow dish, sprinkle pineapple slices (page 70) with brown sugar, a little rum and a grating of fresh ginger. Leave to stand for 30 minutes–3 hours. Grill over medium heat on both sides until golden. Serve drizzled with juices from dish.

grilled pomelo

Cut pomelo in half crossways. Using a sharp knife cut around circumference of each half, then cut between segments to release flesh. Drizzle with maple syrup and dust with ground star anise and ginger. Grill until golden.

grilled snapper & mandarin salad

4 snapper fillets, 185 g (6 oz) each

2 Tbsp chopped fresh coriander

1 Tbsp olive oil

Zest of ½ mandarin orange, plus 4 peeled and segmented mandarins

1 small head cos lettuce, cored and cut into slices

2 spring onions, including tender green parts, thinly sliced

2 sticks of celery, thinly sliced

8–10 caper berries

2 Tbsp lemon juice

Pinch of sugar

Put fish in a shallow dish. Stir together coriander, olive oil, mandarin zest, ½ tsp salt and several grindings of pepper. Brush fish on both sides with coriander mixture. Cover and refrigerate for 15 minutes–4 hours.

In a bowl, combine lettuce, mandarin segments, spring onions, celery and caper berries and toss to mix. Cover and refrigerate.

Build a fire in a charcoal grill for cooking over high heat or preheat a gas grill to 200°C (400°F). Arrange fillets in an oiled grill basket or place on oiled heavy-duty aluminium foil. Place basket on or slide foil onto grill. Grill fillets, turning once, until lightly browned and opaque throughout, about 3 minutes per side.

Add lemon juice and sugar to salad, season with salt and pepper and toss to mix. Taste and adjust seasoning if needed. Divide salad among plates, top each with a fillet and serve at once.

To prepare: 10 minutes, plus 15 minutes to marinate

To cook: 6 minutes

4 servings

swordfish with mango salsa

4 swordfish steaks, each about 185 g (6 oz) and 2.5 cm (1 in) thick

2 tsp grated fresh ginger

1 Tbsp oyster sauce

1 Tbsp grape seed or rape seed oil

1 large, just-ripe mango, peeled, stoned, and finely chopped

1 small red chilli, seeded and finely chopped

2 Tbsp chopped fresh coriander

2 Tbsp lime juice

Put fish steaks in a shallow dish. Stir together ginger, oyster sauce and oil. Pour over fish and turn to coat. Cover and refrigerate for 1–4 hours.

In a small bowl, combine mango, chilli, coriander, lime juice, a pinch of salt and several grindings of pepper and stir to mix well. Cover and refrigerate until ready to serve (it will keep for up to 8 hours). Remove from refrigerator 20 minutes before serving. Taste and adjust seasoning.

Build a fire in a charcoal grill for cooking over medium heat or preheat a gas grill to 180°C (350°F). Arrange fish in an oiled grill basket or on oiled heavy-duty aluminium foil. Place basket on or slide foil onto grill. Grill fish, turning once, until seared and browned but still slightly translucent in the centre, 3–4 minutes per side. Do not overcook. Remove to a platter, tent with foil, and leave to rest for 5 minutes. To serve, place a fish steak on each plate and mound salsa alongside. Serve at once.

To prepare: 10 minutes, plus 1 hour to marinate

To cook: 10 minutes

4 servings

japanese-style grilled sweet potatoes

1 Tbsp sesame seeds

2 or 3 yellow- or orange-fleshed sweet potatoes, about 500 g (1 lb) total, peeled and cut into slices 12 mm (½ in) thick

1 tsp grape seed or rape seed oil

2 tsp white miso

2 tsp firmly packed light brown sugar

1 tsp Asian sesame oil

Build a fire in a charcoal grill for cooking over medium-low heat or preheat a gas grill to 150°C (300°F). Oil grill rack.

Place sesame seeds in a small, dry frying pan over medium heat. Toast, stirring often, until just starting to turn golden, about 2 minutes; watch closely, as they burn easily. Remove at once to a plate. Set aside.

Prick one side of each sweet potato slice with a knife tip. Brush on both sides with grape seed oil. Grill, turning often, until lightly browned and nearly fork-tender, 8–10 minutes. Remove to a serving platter.

Combine grape seed oil, 1–3 Tbsp water (depending on how thick you prefer sauce to be), miso, brown sugar and sesame oil together in a small bowl and stir until sugar and miso dissolve. Drizzle over potatoes and scatter sesame seeds on top. Serve hot, warm, or at room temperature.

To prepare: 10 minutes

To cook: 10 minutes

4 side-dish servings

grilled squash salad

5 or 6 young, slender squashes or yellow courgettes, about 500 g (1 lb)

2 yellow peppers

3 Tbsp olive oil

2 cloves garlic, crushed

1½ tsp Cajun spice mix

2 Tbsp lemon juice

1 small red chilli, seeded and finely chopped

1 spring onion, including tender green parts, thinly sliced

1 tsp fennel seeds, coarsely crushed

60 g (2 oz) crumbled feta cheese

Build a fire in a charcoal grill for cooking over medium-low heat or preheat a gas grill to 150°C (300°F). Oil grill rack.

Cut squashes on diagonal into slices 2 cm (¾ in) thick. Halve and seed peppers and cut into strips 2.5 cm (1 in) wide. Put squash and peppers in a bowl. Add 1 Tbsp olive oil, garlic, spice mix, ½ tsp salt and several grindings of pepper. Turn vegetables to coat evenly.

Grill vegetables, placing long strips perpendicular to grill rack and turning often, until lightly browned and softened, about 8 minutes. Remove to a bowl as they finish cooking.

In a small bowl, whisk together remaining 2 Tbsp olive oil, lemon juice, chilli, spring onion, fennel seeds, ½ tsp salt and several grindings of pepper. Add to bowl with warm vegetables and toss gently to combine. Remove to a serving platter and scatter feta over. Serve warm or at room temperature.

To prepare: 10 minutes

To cook: 8 minutes

4–6 side-dish servings

grilled apricots with sabayon

2 Tbsp orange juice

2 tsp honey

12 apricots, halved and stoned

4 egg yolks

5 Tbsp caster sugar

160 ml (5 fl oz) unsweetened apple juice

Finely grated zest of ½ orange

1–2 tsp orange liqueur such as Cointreau (optional; see Note)

Grape seed or rape seed oil for brushing

Combine orange juice and honey in a small saucepan or in a microwave-proof cup and heat on high for 1–2 minutes on hob top over medium heat or in microwave on high for 30 seconds. Stir to dissolve honey. Pour into a shallow dish and arrange apricot halves, cut side down, in warm syrup. Let stand at room temperature for 30 minutes–4 hours.

Build a fire in a charcoal grill for cooking over medium heat or preheat a gas grill to 180°C (350°F). Oil grill rack.

Drain apricots in a colander set over a stainless-steel bowl to catch their syrup. Set apricots aside. Add egg yolks, sugar, apple juice, orange zest and liqueur, if using, to syrup and whisk to combine. Nest bowl in a saucepan over (but not touching) simmering water. Whisk until mixture has thickened but is fluffy and light and has tripled in volume, 2–3 minutes; there should be no liquid left at bottom of bowl. When you lift whisk, mixture should fall in thick ribbons that hold their shape. Remove from heat.

Brush apricots on both sides with oil and grill until lightly browned and tender, about 3 minutes per side. Serve at once with warm sabayon.

Note: *You can substitute rum or Drambuie for the Cointreau.*

To prepare: 5 minutes, plus 30 minutes to marinate

To cook: 15 minutes

4 dessert servings

rhubarb cranberries red onions

RED FRUITS AND VEGETABLES PROVIDE ANTIOXIDANTS

ruby grapefruit radishes beets

FOR PROTECTION AND HEALING • PROMOTE HEART

cherries watermelon red plums

HEALTH • PROMOTE URINARY TRACT HEALTH • HELP

tomatoes red pears raspberries

REDUCE THE RISK OF CERTAIN CANCERS • IMPROVE

pomegranates red peppers

MEMORY FUNCTION • RED FRUITS AND VEGETABLES

radicchio strawberries quinces

OFFER ANTIOXIDANTS FOR PROTECTION AND HEALING

Red

Red vegetables and fruits—sweet peppers, tomatoes, onions, plums, grapes, cherries, watermelon, blood oranges, chillis, beets, radicchio—offer the cook a vivid palette with which to build dishes that range from scarlet to magenta on dinner plates. There is no doubt that we eat with our eyes, and the showy red family heightens our appetites with its brilliant colours alone.

The varied family of red vegetables and fruits offers countless possibilities for grilling, whether it's plump, grilled cherry tomatoes tossed with basil and mint (page 99), grilled prawns with a watermelon salad, a smoky *romesco* sauce spooned alongside grilled fish, or bright red grilled beet batons dressed in a sweet-and-sour sauce (page 100).

Heralding the start of the summer, fresh cherries, tossed with balsamic vinegar and ginger, make an unexpected and intriguing counterbalance for grilled chicken (page 105). When the season's red plums arrive, make a fresh sauce flavoured with Mediterranean herbs and fruit vinegar to serve with hearty grilled veal chops (page 105).

As the weather cools and appetites seek heartier fare, look to red onions grilled with bacon and calf's liver (page 95) or tender lamb kebabs served on a salad of blood oranges (page 102). No matter which way your flavour preferences lie, you will find that red fruits and vegetables on the grill turn into dishes sure to tempt your appetite.

SPRING	SUMMER	AUTUMN	WINTER
beetroots	cherries	red apples	red apples
redcurrants	red peppers	beetroots	beetroots
pink & red grapefruit	red chillis	red peppers	cranberries
red onions	redcurrants	red chillis	pink & red grapefruit
blood oranges	red onions	cranberries	red grapes
red potatoes	red plums	red grapes	blood oranges
radicchio	radishes	red pears	pomegranates
radishes	raspberries	red plums	red potatoes
rhubarb	strawberries	pomegranates	quinces
strawberries	tomatoes	quinces	radicchio
	watermelon	red potatoes	radishes
		raspberries	

grilled radicchio

2 firm heads radicchio, cores intact, cut into 2.5-cm (1-in) wedges

4 Tbsp extra-virgin olive oil

1 Tbsp lemon juice

1 tsp sugar

125 ml (4 fl oz) balsamic vinegar

60 g (2 oz) Parmesan cheese

Place radicchio in a shallow dish. Add 2 Tbsp olive oil, lemon juice, sugar and a pinch each of salt and pepper. Turn radicchio to coat evenly. Let stand for 30 minutes–4 hours.

Build a fire in a charcoal grill for cooking over medium heat or preheat a gas grill to 180°C (350°F). Oil grill rack.

Put balsamic vinegar in a small saucepan and bring to the boil over medium heat. Reduce heat to medium-low and simmer until reduced by half and the consistency of thick syrup (big bubbles will start rising to surface), 10 minutes. Remove from heat and set aside.

Grill radicchio, turning often, until softened, 5–6 minutes; cores should be translucent and edges lightly browned. Remove to a serving platter. Grate or make shavings of Parmesan cheese. Pour balsamic glaze over radicchio, scatter with Parmesan and drizzle with remaining 2 Tbsp olive oil. Serve radicchio at once.

To prepare: 10 minutes, plus 30 minutes to marinate

To cook: 25 minutes

4–6 side-dish servings

liver & onion bruschetta

2 Tbsp olive oil

60 ml (2 fl oz) red wine

2 cloves garlic, crushed

1 tsp *each* chopped fresh thyme and rosemary

2 bay leaves

2 red onions, sliced into thin rounds

4 strips bacon

250 g (8 oz) calf's liver, trimmed of membrane and cut into strips 12 mm (½ in) wide

6–8 slices country-style bread, cut on diagonal, 2.5 cm (1 in) thick

60 g (2 oz) low-fat sour cream

1½ Tbsp lemon juice

2 tsp Dijon mustard

In a glass measuring jug, whisk together olive oil, wine, garlic, thyme, rosemary and bay leaves and ½ tsp each salt and pepper. Put liver in a dish and pour mixture over, turning to coat evenly. Cover and marinate at room temperature for 20 minutes, or refrigerate for up to 2 hours.

Build a fire in a charcoal grill for cooking over medium heat or preheat a gas grill to 180°C (350°F). Oil grill rack. Arrange onion and bacon strips on grill and cook until onions are browned and softened and bacon is crisp. Remove from grill and set aside. When cool enough to handle, crumble bacon and combine with onions. Oil the grill rack again. Arrange liver on grill and cook until lightly browned on first side, 1½–2 minutes. Turn and cook on second side until browned but still pink in centre, about 2 minutes more. Do not overcook. Remove to a plate. Grill bread slices until lightly browned and grill-marked, about 1 minute per side.

To serve, stir together sour cream, lemon juice and mustard. Divide onions and bacon over toasted bread slices, top with liver and garnish with a spoonful of sour cream mixture. Serve at once.

To prepare: 5 minutes

To cook: 15 minutes

4 starter servings

grilled calamari

1 recipe Romesco Sauce (below)

625 g (1¼ lb) cleaned medium squid, bodies and tentacles separated, rinsed

2 Tbsp olive oil

Zest and juice of 1 lemon

2 grilled or roasted red peppers, peeled, seeded and thinly sliced (optional; page 101)

125 g (4 oz) rocket leaves, tightly packed

Follow recipe below to make *romesco* sauce, and set aside.

Place squid in a bowl. Add olive oil, lemon zest, ½ tsp salt and several grindings of pepper. Turn squid to coat evenly. Cover and refrigerate for at least 30 minutes or up to 4 hours.

Build a fire in a charcoal grill for cooking over high heat or preheat a gas grill to 200°C (400°F). Oil grill rack.

Grill squid in 2 or 3 batches, turning bodies after 1½–2 minutes and tentacles often. Do not crowd grill. Cook just until flesh turns white and is lightly charred, about 1½ minutes more. (The squid bodies will roll up). Remove to a cutting board and cool slightly.

Drizzle lemon juice over squid and cut each rolled squid body diagonally into 3 or 4 slices. If using roasted peppers, combine in a bowl with squid and toss to mix. To serve, divide rocket among plates, arrange squid on top and warm romesco sauce on the side. Serve at once.

To prepare: 15 minutes, plus 30 minutes to marinate

To cook: 15 minutes

4 servings

romesco sauce

2 thick slices country-style bread, crusts removed

4 tomatoes, cored

2 red peppers, seeded and quartered

3 cloves garlic, peeled but left whole

75 g (2½ oz) unsalted roasted almonds

1 small red chilli, halved and seeded

1 tablespoon sherry vinegar or red wine vinegar

1 tsp sugar

Build a fire in a charcoal grill for cooking over medium heat or preheat a gas grill to 180°C (350°F). Oil grill rack.

Grill bread slices until lightly browned and grill-marked, about 1 minute per side. Set aside. Arrange tomatoes, peppers and garlic in oiled grill basket or on oiled heavy-duty aluminium foil. Place basket or slide foil onto grill. Grill, shaking or turning often, until lightly browned and starting to soften, 10–12 minutes. (Remove tomatoes from heat before they start releasing juices; peppers may take another minute or two.) Combine tomatoes, peppers and garlic in a food processor or blender and process until combined. Tear up bread slices and add them along with almonds, chilli, vinegar and sugar. Process to a coarse purée; do not let sauce get too smooth. Season with ½ tsp salt and plenty of ground pepper. Pour into a jug to serve.

Note: Romesco sauce is great with all kinds of grilled seafood and meats. It can be made in advance and stored, covered, in the refrigerator for up to 1 week.

To prepare: 10 minutes

To cook: 12 minutes

3 cups (24 fl oz/750 ml)

prawns with watermelon, feta & mint

500 g (16 oz) large prawns, peeled and deveined, tail intact

1 Tbsp grape seed or rape seed oil

1 tsp red pepper flakes

1 clove garlic, crushed

2 Tbsp lime zest

½ tsp garam masala

750 g (1½ lb) watermelon

3 Tbsp lime juice

4 fresh mint leaves, thinly sliced

4 iceberg lettuce leaves

125 g (4 oz) feta cheese, cut into 12-mm (½-in) cubes

2 Tbsp pine nuts, toasted (page 27)

Put prawns in a bowl. Add oil, red pepper flakes, garlic, lime zest, garam masala, ½ tsp salt and several grindings of pepper. Turn to coat prawns evenly. Cover and refrigerate for 30 minutes–4 hours.

Peel and seed watermelon; cut into 2.5-cm (1-in) chunks. Combine watermelon, 2 Tbsp lime juice and mint in a bowl. Toss to coat watermelon evenly. Cover and refrigerate until ready to serve; it will keep for up to 3 hours.

Build a fire in a charcoal grill for cooking over high heat or preheat a gas grill to 200°C (400°F). Oil grill rack. Drain prawns and grill, turning often, until opaque throughout, 3–4 minutes. Remove to a platter and drizzle with remaining 1 Tbsp lime juice.

Line bowls with lettuce leaves. Divide watermelon salad among bowls, scatter feta and pine nuts over, and pile on the hot prawns and serve.

To prepare: 15 minutes, plus 30 minutes to marinate

To cook: 3 minutes

4 servings

grilled cherry tomatoes

470 g (15 oz) cherry tomatoes

3 tsp extra-virgin olive oil

½ tsp sugar

15 g (½ oz) loosely packed basil leaves, torn

12 fresh mint leaves, thinly sliced

1 tsp balsamic vinegar

Build a fire in a charcoal grill for cooking over medium-high heat or preheat a gas grill to 190°C (375°F).

Put tomatoes in a bowl. Add 1 tsp olive oil, sugar, ½ tsp salt and several grindings of pepper and toss to coat evenly.

Put tomatoes in an oiled grill basket and place basket on grill. Grill, shaking often, until tomatoes are softened and lightly browned and skins are starting to split, about 3 minutes. Do not cook until fully collapsed. Return tomatoes to bowl and toss with herbs, vinegar, and remaining 2 tsp olive oil. Serve warm or at room temperature.

To prepare: 5 minutes

To cook: 3 minutes

4–6 side-dish servings

grilled chilli sauce

Grill 1 red chilli and 1 red pepper until blackened, then peel and seed. Boil 180 ml (6 fl oz) rice vinegar with 125 g (4 oz) sugar for 5 minutes. Purée peppers with syrup. Use as dipping sauce for chicken or pork.

sweet & sour beetroots

Cut peeled beetroots into large matchsticks and toss with olive oil to coat. Arrange in a basket and grill until tender, shaking often. Season with a little sugar and sherry vinegar, salt and pepper. Toss with oregano leaves and garnish with feta.

grilled red peppers

Grill whole peppers over high heat, turning until charred all over. Cover and cool, then peel. Slice flesh into strips, discarding seeds and season. Combine equal parts pesto and extra-virgin olive oil and drizzle over peppers.

red onions with fennel

Cut red onions into thick rounds. Brush with olive oil and grill over medium heat until browned and softened, 8–10 minutes. Drizzle with honey and sprinkle with red wine vinegar and toasted fennel seeds. Serve with grilled meats.

lamb kebabs with blood orange salad

500 g (1 lb) boneless lamb steaks or fillets, cut into 2.5-cm (1-in) cubes

1 Tbsp olive oil

Zest of 1 blood orange

1½ tsp ground cumin

1 tsp ground coriander

½ tsp red pepper flakes

1 tsp dried oregano

4 blood oranges, peeled and sliced crossways into thin rounds

10-cm (4-in) piece cucumber, thinly sliced

2 avocados, stoned, peeled and cut into 12-mm (½-in) chunks

2 spring onions, including tender green parts, thinly sliced

2 Tbsp lime juice

2 Tbsp chopped fresh coriander

Put lamb in a bowl. Add olive oil, orange zest, 1 tsp cumin, ground coriander, red pepper flakes, oregano, ½ tsp salt and several grindings of pepper. Turn lamb to coat evenly. Cover and marinate at room temperature for at least 30 minutes, or refrigerate for up to 4 hours. Remove from refrigerator 20 minutes before cooking.

Soak 8 wooden skewers in water to cover for 30 minutes. Build a fire in a charcoal grill for cooking over medium-high heat or preheat a gas grill to 190°C (375°F). Oil grill rack.

Layer oranges, cucumber, avocados and spring onions on a serving platter. Drizzle with lime juice, sprinkle with remaining ½ tsp cumin and season with salt and pepper.

Thread lamb onto skewers. Grill, turning often, until lightly browned and tender, about 5 minutes. Remove to a platter, tent with foil and leave to rest for 5 minutes.

To serve, divide salad among plates and top each with 2 lamb kebabs. Sprinkle with coriander and serve at once.

To prepare: 15 minutes, plus 30 minutes to marinate

To cook: 5 minutes

4 servings

veal chops with red plum sauce

4 veal loin chops, about 310 g (10 oz) each

2 Tbsp olive oil

1½ Tbsp fruit vinegar such as plum or raspberry

2 shallots, finely chopped

2 tsp *each* finely chopped fresh thyme, oregano and rosemary

4 large, firm red plums, stoned and finely diced

2 tsp sugar

Put veal chops in a shallow dish. In a small bowl, stir together olive oil, vinegar, shallots, herbs, 1 tsp salt and several grindings of pepper. Brush veal on both sides with half of herb mixture; put remainder in a small saucepan. Cover veal and leave at room temperature for 30 minutes, or refrigerate for up to 6 hours. Bring to room temperature before grilling.

Build a fire in a charcoal grill for cooking over medium-high heat or preheat a gas grill to 190°C (375°F). Oil grill rack. Grill veal until nicely browned on the first side, about 3½ minutes. Turn and cook other side for 1½–2 minutes more for medium-rare (a meat thermometer inserted in thickest part, away from bone, should read 54°C/135°F). Remove to a platter, tent with foil and leave to rest for 5 minutes.

While veal is resting, add plums and sugar to saucepan with herb mixture and bring to the boil, stirring, just to soften plums. Remove from heat. To serve, put a veal chop on each warmed plate and spoon warm plum sauce over. Serve at once.

To prepare: 10 minutes, plus 30 minutes to marinate

To cook: 6 minutes

4 servings

chicken with cherry salsa

4 skinless, boneless chicken breasts, 150 g (5 oz) each

4 Tbsp balsamic vinegar

2 tsp light brown sugar

1½ tsp finely grated fresh ginger

6 whole fresh mint leaves, plus 5 leaves torn into small pieces

250 g (8 oz) cherries, stoned and finely chopped

1 Tbsp grape seed or rape seed oil

1 tsp sugar

Place chicken between 2 pieces of cling film. Using a meat pounder, pound to an even thickness. Sprinkle with 3 Tbsp vinegar, brown sugar, 1 tsp ginger, whole mint leaves, ½ tsp salt and several grindings of fresh pepper. Turn to coat evenly, cover and refrigerate for 30 minutes–4 hours. Remove from refrigerator 15 minutes before cooking.

Combine cherries, oil, remaining 1 Tbsp vinegar, torn mint, sugar and remaining ½ tsp ginger in a bowl and toss to make a salsa. Stand for at least 30 minutes, or cover and refrigerate for up to 4 hours. Bring to room temperature before serving. Taste and adjust seasoning.

Build a fire in a charcoal grill for cooking over medium heat or preheat a gas grill to 180°C (350°F). Oil grill rack. Grill chicken, more attractive side down, until golden, about 8 minutes. Turn, cover grill and cook until chicken feels springy to the touch and juices run clear when pierced in the thickest part, about 5 minutes more. Remove to a platter, tent with foil, and leave to rest for 10 minutes. Serve warm with the salsa.

To prepare: 15 minutes, plus 30 minutes to marinate

To cook: 10 minutes, plus 10 minutes to rest

4 servings

caramelised red pears with cinnamon

250 ml (8 fl oz) red wine

185 ml (6 fl oz) honey

1 tsp cinnamon

1 tsp finely grated fresh ginger

4 just-ripe red pears, quartered and cored, each quarter cut in half lengthways

1 tsp butter

Combine wine, honey, cinnamon and ginger in a saucepan and bring to the boil over medium-high heat. Boil for 5 minutes. Remove from heat and add sliced pears, turning to coat evenly. Leave to macerate at room temperature, turning occasionally, for 30 minutes.

Build a fire in a charcoal grill for cooking over medium heat or preheat a gas grill to 180°C (350°F). Oil grill rack.

Use a slotted spoon to lift pears from liquid and pour the liquid into a small pot. Bring the liquid to the boil over high heat, skimming any foam that may form on surface. Add butter and boil, stirring occasionally until mixture starts to form large bubbles, is reduced by half and is thick and syrupy, about 5 minutes.

Grill pears until they are lightly caramelised, about 2 minutes per side.

Divide pears among serving plates, allowing 1 whole pear (8 slices) per serving. Drizzle with reduced syrup and serve.

To prepare: 10 minutes, plus 30 minutes to macerate

To cook: 9 minutes

4 dessert servings

grilled grapes in yoghurt & sour cream

375 g (12 oz) seedless red grapes

185 g (6 oz) low-fat sour cream

75 g (2½ oz) plain low-fat or whole yoghurt

1 tsp vanilla extract

Zest of ½ orange

105 g (3½ oz) firmly packed light brown sugar

Arrange grapes in a single layer in a shallow flameproof baking or gratin dish; they should fit tightly. Stir sour cream, yoghurt, vanilla and orange zest together in a small bowl. Spread sour cream mixture evenly over grapes and sprinkle brown sugar on top. Refrigerate for 30 minutes–4 hours.

Preheat grill.

Slide grapes in baking dish under grill about 10 cm (4 in) from heat source and grill until mixture bubbles and sugar starts to caramelise, about 5 minutes. Serve hot.

To prepare: 5 minutes, plus 30 minutes to macerate

To cook: 5 minutes

4 dessert servings

soybeans brown rice chick peas

WHOLE GRAINS, LEGUMES, SEEDS, AND NUTS PROMOTE

pecans chestnuts bulgur wheat

ARTERY AND HEART HEALTH • HELP REDUCE THE RISK

flaxseed sesame seeds polenta

OF DIABETES • REDUCE HIGH BLOOD PRESSURE • OFFER

pumpkin seeds cashews quinoa

ANTIOXIDANTS FOR PROTECTION AND HEALING • HELP

kasha macadamia nuts walnuts

REDUCE THE RISK OF STROKE • MAY REDUCE THE RISK

hazelnuts oats couscous millet

OF CANCERS OF THE BREAST, PROSTATE AND COLON

Brown

Whole grains, beans and peas, nuts, seeds—these nutritional powerhouses have a chameleon ability to take on different tastes and textures, depending on how they are prepared. They are not typically grilled, but they are excellent companions to all kinds of grilled foods, delivering wonderful flavour along with a wealth of vitamins and photonutrients that are critical to a healthy lifestyle.

The toothsome texture of grains and legumes makes them the ideal base for healthful salads, such as bulgur with grilled courgette, asparagus, and spring onion (page 123); cannellini beans, capers, sun-dried tomatoes and basil topped with grilled tuna (page 117); or grilled rice patties with Asian flavours (page 118).

Pulses like beans and peas and grains are also transformed into creamy purées, evidence of the versatility of this varied group's members. For example, tinned butter beans are blended with lemon, garlic, feta and herbs until smooth and then served with grilled chicken thighs (page 114), or creamy polenta is allowed to set and then cut into squares, grilled until browned, and served with a mushroom ragout (page 113).

To satisfy your sweet tooth, look to bananas grilled in their skins and then topped with nature's most delectable brown seeds: dark chocolate and nuts (page 124). And you thought that food that was both healthy and decadent was a contradiction!

GRAINS	LEGUMES	SEEDS	NUTS
amaranth	black beans	flaxseed	almonds
barley	cannellini beans	pumpkin seeds	Brazil nuts
bulgur wheat	chickpeas	sesame seeds	cashews
couscous	cranberry beans	sunflower seeds	chestnuts
kasha (buckwheat groats)	kidney beans		hazelnuts
millet	butter beans		macadamia nuts
oats	soybeans		pecans
polenta	black-eyed peas		pine nuts
quinoa	split peas		pistachio nuts
brown rice	lentils		walnuts
whole wheat	peanuts		

grilled polenta with mushroom ragout

220 g (7 oz) instant polenta

125 g (4 oz) blue cheese, crumbled

Zest of ½ lemon

3 Tbsp butter

750 g (1½ lb) cremini mushrooms, brushed clean, stemmed and thinly sliced

2 cloves garlic, crushed

3 Tbsp chopped fresh basil

2 Tbsp lemon juice

125 ml (4 fl oz) chicken stock

1 tsp cornflour

60 g (2 oz) walnut pieces, chopped

Line a 21.5-cm (12-in) baking pan with baking paper.

Bring 1.25 litres (40 fl oz) water, 2 tsp salt and several grindings of pepper to the boil in a saucepan over medium-high heat. Add polenta in a thin stream, stirring constantly. Cover and cook until grains are tender and mixture starts to pull away from sides of pan, 3–5 minutes. Remove from heat, add cheese and lemon zest and stir until cheese is melted. Pour into prepared pan, spread evenly with a rubber spatula, and leave to cool for about 40 minutes, and then refrigerate until firm, 30–40 minutes more.

Preheat grill and butter a baking sheet. Melt butter in a frying pan over medium heat. Add mushrooms and garlic and cook until mushrooms are softened and starting to release their liquids, about 5 minutes. Add basil, lemon juice, stock mixed with cornflour, ½ tsp salt and several grindings of pepper and cook until mushrooms are tender and sauce is lightly thickened, 3–4 minutes more.

Toast walnuts in a small, dry frying pan over medium heat, shaking occasionally, until they start to brown and become fragrant, 3–4 minutes. Remove from heat.

Cut polenta into 10-cm (4-in) rounds and arrange on prepared baking sheet. Slide under grill 10–15 cm (4–6 ins) from heat source and grill until lightly browned, about 5 minutes. Divide polenta rounds among warmed plates. Spoon mushroom mixture on top and scatter with walnuts to garnish. Serve at once.

Note: Cover and refrigerate the cooked polenta for up to 3 days.

To prepare: 10 minutes, plus 70 minutes to cool and chill

To cook: 25 minutes

5–6 servings

chicken thighs with butter bean purée

750 g (1½ lb) skin intact, boneless
chicken thighs

Zest and juice of 1 lemon

2 tsp olive oil

1 tsp dried oregano

¼ tsp red pepper flakes

Butter Bean Purée
2 Tbsp olive oil

1 clove garlic, finely chopped

Zest of ½ lemon, plus zest
for garnish

2 tins (410 g/13 oz each) butter beans
rinsed and drained

125 g (4 oz) feta cheese,
crumbled

2 tsp chopped fresh marjoram, plus
sprigs for garnish

Put chicken in a bowl. Add lemon zest and juice, olive oil, oregano, red pepper flakes, 1 tsp salt and several grindings of pepper. Turn chicken to coat evenly. Cover and refrigerate for 30 minutes–12 hours. Remove from refrigerator 30 minutes before grilling.

For Bean Purée: Combine olive oil, garlic and lemon zest in a medium saucepan and place over medium heat until they sizzle. Add beans and 80 ml (3 fl oz) water and cook for 3–4 minutes to infuse flavours, reducing heat if necessary to avoid scorching. Alternatively, combine olive oil, garlic and lemon zest in a heatproof bowl and microwave on high for 30 seconds. Stir in beans and water. Cover, return to microwave for 4 minutes. Remove from heat, add feta and chopped marjoram, and purée until smooth in a food mill or food processor. Spoon back into a saucepan or microwave-safe bowl and set aside.

Build a fire in a charcoal grill for cooking over medium-low heat or preheat a gas grill to 150°C (300°F). Oil grill rack. Grill chicken, skin side down, turning once, until browned on both sides and opaque throughout, about 12 minutes. Remove to a platter, tent with foil and stand for 5 minutes. While chicken is resting, gently reheat bean purée in saucepan on hob top for 3–4 minutes or in microwave in microwave-safe bowl, 1–2 minutes.

To serve, spoon bean purée on to warmed plates and top with chicken. Garnish with marjoram sprigs and a little lemon zest.

To prepare: 15 minutes,
plus 30 minutes to marinate

To cook: 20 minutes

4 servings

grilled tuna with cannellini bean salad

4 tuna steaks, each about 185 g (6 oz) and 2.5 cm (1 in) thick

Zest of ½ lemon

1 tsp finely chopped fresh rosemary

Cannellini Bean Salad

4 oil-packed sun-dried tomatoes, drained and thinly sliced

3 Tbsp extra-virgin olive oil

2 Tbsp lemon juice

2 small cloves garlic, finely chopped

2 Tbsp tiny capers, rinsed and drained

2 tins (410 g/13 oz each) cannellini beans, rinsed and drained

250 g (8 oz) cherry tomatoes, halved

75 g (2½ oz) oil-cured black olives such as Niçoise, stoned if desired

2 Tbsp torn fresh basil leaves or chopped fresh parsley

Arrange tuna in a single layer in a shallow dish and brush both sides with olive oil. Sprinkle with lemon zest, rosemary, ½ tsp salt and several grindings of pepper. Cover and refrigerate for 1–4 hours. Remove from the refrigerator 15 minutes before cooking.

For Bean Salad: In a saucepan or heatproof bowl, combine sun-dried tomatoes, olive oil, lemon juice, garlic and capers. Mix in beans, cover and heat over medium-low heat for several minutes until liquid is absorbed. Alternatively, microwave on high in a heatproof bowl for 3–4 minutes. Leave to cool, then add cherry tomatoes, olives and basil and toss to distribute evenly. Season with salt and pepper.

Preheat the grill. Place fish on an aluminium foil-lined baking sheet and slide under the grill 10 cm (4 in) from heat source. Grill, turning once, until fish is browned but still pink in the centre, 2–3 minutes per side. Do not overcook. Remove to a platter, tent with foil, and rest for 5 minutes.

To serve, divide bean salad among individual plates and top each portion with a tuna steak.

To prepare: 10 minutes, plus 1 hour to marinate

To cook: 5 minutes

4 servings

prawns, beans & tomatoes

Toss prawns with salt, pepper, olive oil and finely chopped chilli and garlic. Grill over medium heat until pink. Toss with rinsed tinned haricot beans, chopped tomatoes and spring onions. Dress with a garlicky herbed lemon juice vinaigrette.

grilled rice patties with asian flavours

Coarsely purée 155 g (5 oz) cooked brown rice with 1 egg, grated ginger and soy sauce. Stir in sliced spring onion and grated carrot. Form into small patties and cook on a lightly oiled pan on a grill until set and lightly browned.

red kidney bean quesadillas

Spread a flour tortilla with chilli sauce. Top with rinsed tinned kidney beans and sprinkle with shredded mozzarella, chopped fresh coriander, salt and pepper. Top with a tortilla and grill on both sides until golden and melted.

chickpeas with baby spinach

In a baking dish, toss 750 g (24 oz) rinsed tinned chickpeas and 2 thinly sliced tomatoes with 2 Tbsp olive oil, salt and pepper. Grill until top is browned. Toss while still warm with baby spinach and lemon juice.

grilled pepper & quinoa salad

185 g (6 oz) quinoa (see Note)

Grilled Peppers
2 red peppers

2 yellow peppers

1 medium tomato, coarsely chopped

Zest of 1 lemon

1 clove garlic, chopped

15 g (½ oz) loosely packed fresh basil leaves, plus torn leaves for garnish

1 tsp sherry vinegar or white wine vinegar

1 Tbsp extra-virgin olive oil

2 Tbsp lemon juice

Preheat grill.

Toast quinoa in a dry frying pan over medium heat, stirring, until it starts to smell nutty, 2–3 minutes. Remove to a fine-mesh sieve and rinse under cold running water until water runs clear. Drain thoroughly and place in a pot with 750 ml (24 fl oz) water. Bring to the boil, then reduce heat to low, cover and simmer until water is absorbed and grains are translucent, about 15 minutes. Remove quinoa from heat, fluff and cool completely.

For Grilled Peppers: Place peppers on a baking sheet and slide under grill about 10 cm (4 in) from heat source. Grill, turning often, until skin is blackened on all sides, about 15 minutes. Remove to a covered bowl or seal in a paper bag. Leave peppers to steam until cool, about 10 minutes. Rub and peel off charred skins. Cut peppers, reserving juices, in half lengthways, remove seeds and membranes and chop finely.

In a blender or food processor, combine reserved juice from peppers, lemon zest, tomato, garlic, ½ cup basil, vinegar, olive oil, 2 Tbsp water, 1 tsp salt and several grindings of pepper and purée until smooth to make a dressing. Add to cooled quinoa along with peppers, lemon juice and zest and toss until evenly combined. Season with additional salt and pepper to taste.

To serve, mound on a platter or divide among plates and garnish with torn basil. Serve at room temperature.

Note: You need to rinse quinoa to remove any bitter-flavored saponin residue. Most of this natural coating is removed by commercial processing, but some can remain. Put the quinoa in a fine-mesh sieve and rinse well while gently rubbing the grains between your fingers.

To prepare: 10 minutes

To cook: 18 minutes

4–6 servings

bulgur salad with courgettes, asparagus & spring onions

8–10 spears asparagus, tough ends snapped off

2 courgettes, cut on diagonal into slices 6 mm (¼ in) thick

Boiling water as needed

1 tsp extra-virgin olive oil

280 g (9 oz) bulgur wheat

Dressing

3 Tbsp extra-virgin olive oil

2 tsp lemon zest

2 Tbsp lemon juice

2 tsp ground cumin

½ tsp turmeric

½ tsp cardamom seeds, crushed

220 g (7 oz) drained cooked or tinned chickpeas

2 spring onions, including tender green parts, thinly sliced

30 fresh mint leaves, finely chopped

2 Tbsp finely chopped fresh parsley

Build a fire in a charcoal grill for cooking over medium heat or preheat a gas grill to 180°C (350°F). Oil grill rack.

Put asparagus and courgettes in a heatproof bowl, pour boiling water over them to cover, and stand for 2 minutes to soften slightly. Drain, cool, and toss with 1 tsp olive oil.

When grill is ready, put bulgur in a heatproof bowl and add boiling water to cover by 5 cm (2 in). Stand for 10 minutes. Meanwhile, grill asparagus and courgettes, placing them perpendicular to grill rack and turning often, until lightly browned and tender-crisp, 4–5 minutes. Remove to a platter and cool slightly. Cut asparagus spears on diagonal into thirds.

For Dressing: In a medium bowl, whisk together 3 Tbsp olive oil, lemon zest and juice, cumin, turmeric, cardamom, 1 tsp salt and several grindings of pepper.

Stir chickpeas into bowl with dressing and then microwave on high in a microwave safe bowl for 1 minute to blend flavours. Alternatively, heat chickpeas with dressing in a saucepan over medium heat for a couple of minutes, stirring occasionally. Drain bulgur. Combine grilled vegetables, bulgur, spring onions, mint, parsley and chickpeas with dressing in a serving bowl and toss to distribute and coat evenly. Serve warm or at room temperature.

To prepare: 20 minutes

To cook: 5 minutes

6 side-dish servings

grilled bananas with nuts & chocolate

4 just-ripe bananas, skins on, ends trimmed

60 g (2 oz) good-quality plain chocolate, coarsely chopped

30 g (1 oz) chopped unsalted pecans

Build a fire in a charcoal grill for cooking over medium heat or preheat a gas grill to 180°C (350°F). Oil grill rack.

Grill bananas in their skins, turning often, until skins are blackened on both sides and bananas have softened, 8–10 minutes. Remove to a cutting board.

Place chocolate in a microwave-safe bowl and microwave on high for 1½ minutes. Stir as needed to complete the melting. Alternatively, place chocolate in a heatproof bowl or the top pan of a double boiler and place over a pan containing, but not touching, 2.5 cm (1 in) water. Bring water to simmering point over medium heat and melt chocolate, stirring occasionally, about 4 minutes.

Meanwhile, toast pecans in a small, dry frying pan over medium heat, shaking occasionally, until they start to brown and smell aromatic, 3–4 minutes. Remove from heat.

Peel bananas, slice on a bias, and place on 4 serving plates. Drizzle peeled bananas with melted chocolate and scatter with nuts.

Note: Accompany with frozen vanilla yoghurt or mango sorbet, if desired.

To prepare: 5 minutes

To cook: 15 minutes

4 dessert servings

Nutrients at work

Humans need more than forty nutrients to support life. Many foods are good sources of these various nutrients, but no single food provides everything. Eating a variety of foods, preferably in their whole form, is the best way to get all the nutrients your body needs. Some nutrients require others for optimal absorption, but excessive amounts may result in health problems.

Until recently, nutritionists believed that the distribution of carbohydrates, protein and fat in a healthy diet to be 55 percent of calories from carbohydrates, 15 percent of calories from protein, and 30 percent of calories from fat. As we have learned more about individual health needs and differences in our metabolism, we have become more flexible in determining what will constitute a well-balanced diet. The table below shows macronutrient ranges recommended in September 2002 by the Institute of Medicine, part of the U.S. National Academies. These ranges are more likely to accommodate everyone's health needs. To help you evaluate and balance your diet as you prepare the recipes in this book, turn to pages 130–33 for nutritional analyses of each recipe. Nutrition experts have also determined guidelines for vitamins and minerals. For more information, see pages 128–29.

CARBOHYDRATES, PROTEIN AND FATS

NUTRIENTS AND FOOD SOURCES	FUNCTIONS	RECOMMENDED % OF DAILY CALORIES AND GUIDANCE
Carbohydrates COMPLEX CARBOHYDRATES • Grains, breads, cereals, pastas • Dried beans and peas, lentils • Starchy vegetables (potatoes, corn, green peas)	• Main source of energy for the body • Particularly important for the brain and nervous system • Fibre aids normal digestion	45–65% • Favour complex carbohydrates, especially legumes, vegetables and whole grains (brown rice; whole-grain bread, pasta and cereal). • Many foods high in complex carbohydrates are also good fibre sources. Among the best are bran cereals, tinned and dried beans, dried fruit and rolled oats. Recommended daily intake of fibre for adults under age 50 is 25 g for women and 38 g for men. For women over age 50, intake is 21 g; for men, 30 g.
SIMPLE CARBOHYDRATES • Naturally occurring sugars in fruits, vegetables and milk • Added refined sugars in soft drinks, sweets, baked goods, jams and jellies, etc.	• Provide energy	• Fruit and vegetables have naturally occurring sugars but also have vitamins, minerals and phytochemicals. Refined sugar, on the other hand, has little to offer in the way of nutrition, so limit your intake to get the most from your daily calories.

Source: Institute of Medicine. Dietary Reference Intakes for Energy, Carbohydrates, Fiber, Fat, Protein, and Amino Acids (Macronutrients).

NUTRIENTS AND FOOD SOURCES	FUNCTIONS	RECOMMENDED % OF DAILY CALORIES AND GUIDANCE
Protein • Foods from animal sources • Dried beans and peas, nuts • Grain products	• Builds and repairs cells • Regulates body processes by providing components for enzymes, hormones, fluid balance, nerve transmission	10–35% • Choose lean sources such as dried beans, fish, poultry, lean cuts of meat, soy and low-fat dairy products most of the time. • Egg yolks are rich in many nutrients but also high in cholesterol; limit to 5 per week.
Fats All fats are mixtures of saturated and unsaturated (polyunsaturated and monounsaturated) types. Polyunsaturated and especially monounsaturated types are more desirable because they promote cardiovascular health.	• Supply essential fatty acids needed for various body processes and to build cell membranes, particularly of the brain and nervous system • Transport certain vitamins	20–35% • Experts disagree about the ideal amount of total fat in the diet. Some say more is fine if it is heart-healthy fat; others recommend limiting total fat. Virtually all experts agree that saturated fat, trans fats, and cholesterol, all of which can raise "bad" (LDL) cholesterol, should be limited.
PRIMARILY SATURATED • Foods from animal sources (meat fat, butter, cheese, cream) • Coconut, palm, palm kernel oils	• Raises blood levels of "bad" (LDL) cholesterol	• Limit saturated fat.
PRIMARILY POLYUNSATURATED (PUFA) • Omega-3 fatty acids: herring, salmon, mackerel, lake trout, sardines, sword-fish, nuts, flaxseed, rape seed oil, soy-bean oil, tofu • Omega-6: vegetable oils such as corn, soybean, and safflower	• Reduces inflammation; influences blood clotting and blood vessel activity to improve blood flow	• Eat fish at least twice a week. • Substitute PUFA for saturated fat or trans fat when possible.
PRIMARILY MONOUNSATURATED (MUFA) Olive oil, rape seed oil, sesame oil, avocados, almonds, chicken fat	• Raises blood levels of "good" (HDL) cholesterol	• Substitute MUFA for saturated fat or trans fat when possible.
DIETARY CHOLESTEROL Foods from animal sources (egg yolks, organ meats, cheese, fish roe, meat)	• A structural component of cell membranes and some hormones	• The body makes cholesterol, and some foods contain dietary cholesterol.
TRANS FAT Processed foods, purchased baked goods, margarine and shortening	• Raises blood levels of "bad" (LDL) cholesterol	• Limit trans fat.

FAT-SOLUBLE VITAMINS AND FOOD SOURCES	FUNCTIONS	DAILY RECOMMENDED INTAKES FOR ADULTS*
Vitamin A Dairy products, deep yellow-orange fruits and vegetables, dark green leafy vegetables, liver, fish, fortified milk, cheese, butter	• Promotes growth and healthy skin and hair • Helps build strong bones and teeth • Works as an antioxidant that may reduce the risk of some cancers and other diseases • Helps night vision • Increases immunity	700 mcg for women 900 mcg for men
Vitamin D Fortified milk, salmon, sardines, herring, butter, liver, fortified cereals, fortified margarine	• Builds bones and teeth • Enhances calcium and phosphorus absorption and regulates blood levels of these nutrients	5–10 mcg
Vitamin E Nuts and seeds, vegetable and seed oils (corn, soybean, sunflower), whole-grain breads and cereals, dark green leafy vegetables, dried beans and peas	• Helps form red blood cells • Improves immunity • Prevents oxidation of "bad" LDL cholesterol • Works as an antioxidant that may reduce the risk of some cancers	15 mg
Vitamin K Dark green leafy vegetables, carrots, asparagus, cauliflower, cabbage, liver, wheat bran, wheat germ, eggs	• Needed for normal blood clotting • Promotes protein synthesis for bone, plasma and organs	90 mcg for women 120 mcg for men

WATER-SOLUBLE VITAMINS

B vitamins Grain products, dried beans and peas, dark green leafy vegetables, dairy products, meat, poultry, fish, eggs, organ meats, milk, brewer's yeast, wheat germ, seeds	• Helps the body use carbohydrates (biotin, B_{12}, niacin, pantothenic acid) • Regulate metabolism of cells and energy production (niacin, pantothenic acid) • Keep the nerves and muscles healthy (thiamin) • Protect against spinal birth defects (folate) • Protect against heart disease (B_6, folate)	• B_6: 1.3–1.5 mg • B_{12}: 2.4 mcg • Biotin: 30 mcg • Niacin: 14 mg niacin equivalents for women; 16 mg for men • Pantothenic acid: 5 mg • Riboflavin: 1.1 mg for women; 1.3 mg for men • Thiamin: 1.1 mg for women; 1.2 mg for men • Folate: 400 mcg
Vitamin C Many fruits and vegetables, especially citrus fruits, broccoli, tomatoes, green peppers, melons, strawberries, potatoes, papayas	• Helps build body tissues • Fights infection and helps heal wounds • Helps body absorb iron and folate • Helps keep gums healthy • Works as an antioxidant	75 mg for women 90 mg for men

Sources: Institute of Medicine reports, 1999–2001

*mcg=micrograms; mg=milligrams

MINERALS** AND FOOD SOURCES	FUNCTIONS	DAILY RECOMMENDED INTAKES FOR ADULTS*
Calcium Dairy products (especially hard cheese, yoghurt, and milk), fortified juices, sardines and tinned fish eaten with bones, shellfish, tofu (if processed with calcium), dark green leafy vegetables	• Helps build bones and teeth and keep them strong • Helps heart, muscles and nerves work properly	1,000–1,200 mg
Iron Meat, fish, shellfish, egg yolks, dark green leafy vegetables, dried beans and peas, grain products, dried fruits	• Helps red blood cells carry oxygen • Component of enzymes • Strengthens immune system	18 mg for women 8 mg for men
Magnesium Nuts and seeds, whole-grain products, dark green leafy vegetables, dried beans and peas	• Helps build bones and teeth • Helps nerves and muscles work properly • Necessary for DNA and RNA • Necessary for carbohydrate metabolism	310–320 mg for women 400–420 mg for men
Phosphorus Seeds and nuts, meat, poultry, fish, dried beans and peas, dairy products, whole-grain products, eggs, brewer's yeast	• Helps build strong bones and teeth • Has many metabolic functions • Helps body get energy from food	700 mg
Potassium Fruit, vegetables, dried beans and peas, meat, poultry, fish, dairy products, whole grains	• Helps body maintain water and mineral balance • Regulates heartbeat and blood pressure	2,000 mg suggested; no official recommended intake
Selenium Mushrooms, seafood, chicken, organ meats, brown rice, wholemeal bread, peanuts, onions	• Works as an antioxidant with vitamin E to protect cells from damage • Boosts immune function	55 mg
Zinc Oysters, meat, poultry, fish, soybeans, nuts, whole grains, wheat germ	• Helps body metabolise proteins, carbohydrates and alcohol • Helps wounds heal • Needed for growth, immune response and reproduction	8 mg for women 11 mg for men

** The following minerals are generally sufficient in the diet when the minerals listed above are present: chloride, chromium, copper, fluoride, iodine, manganese, molybdenum, sodium, and sulfur. For information on functions and food sources, consult a nutrition book.

Nutritional values

The recipes in this book have been analysed for significant nutrients to help you evaluate your diet and balance your meals throughout the day. Using these calculations, along with the other information in this book, you can create meals that have the optimal balance of nutrients. Having the following nutritional values at your fingertips will help you plan more healthy meals.

Keep in mind that the calculations reflect nutrients per serving unless otherwise noted. Not included in the calculations are optional ingredients or those added to taste, or that are suggested as an alternative or used as a substitution in the recipe, recipe note, or variation. For recipes that yield a range of servings, the calculations are for the middle of that range. Many recipes call for a specific amount of salt and also suggest seasoning food to taste; however, if you are on a low-sodium diet, it is prudent to omit salt. If you have particular concerns about any nutrient needs, consult your doctor.

The numbers for all nutritional values have been rounded using the guidelines required for reporting nutrient levels in the "Nutrition Facts" panel on food labels.

The best way to acquire the nutrients your body needs is through food. However, a balanced multivitamin-mineral supplement or a fortified cereal that does not exceed 100 percent of the daily need for any nutrient is a safe addition to your diet.

WHAT COUNTS AS A SERVING?	HOW MANY SERVINGS DO YOU NEED EACH DAY?		
	For a 1,600-calorie-per-day diet *(children 2–6, sedentary women, some older adults)*	For a 2,200-calorie-per-day diet *(children over 6, teen girls, active women, sedentary men)*	For a 2,800-calorie-per-day diet *(teen boys, active men)*
Fruit Group 1 medium whole fruit such as apple, orange, banana, or pear 60–90 g (2–3 oz) chopped, cooked or tinned fruit 90 g (3 oz) dried fruit 180 ml (6 fl oz) fruit juice	2	3	4
Vegetable Group 30 g (1 oz) raw, leafy vegetables 60–90 g (2–3 oz) other vegetables, cooked or raw 180 ml (6 fl oz) vegetable juice	3	4	5
Bread, Cereal, Rice and Pasta Group 1 slice of bread 180 g (6 oz) ready-to-eat cereal 80 g (2.5 oz) cooked cereal, rice, pasta	6	9	11

Adapted from USDA Dietary Guidelines (2005).

Purple & blue		CALORIES	PROTEIN/ GM	CARBS/ GM	TOT. FAT/ GM	SAT. FAT/ GM	CHOL/ MG	FIBRE/ GM	SODIUM/ MG
p.23	Grilled aubergine & feta cheese rolls	153	8	9	11	5	13	4	470
p.23	Scallops with pepper dressing	163	10	5	11	2	19	1	95
p.24	Grilled pizzas with blue potatoes & onions	359	13	41	16	6	26	2	389
p.27	Fig & purple endive salad	168	1	17	12	1	0	3	231
p.27	Halibut & purple grapes	227	36	6	6	2	59	0	529
p.30	Grilled salmon with purple asparagus slaw	427	43	13	23	3	107	4	243
p.33	Chicken, aubergine & tomato salad	464	39	16	27	4	94	7	738
p.33	Chicken & fig kebabs	354	32	23	15	4	116	5	105
p.34	Grilled plums with kirsch cream	214	2	17	16	10	58	1	15
p.34	Grilled berry parcels	159	2	39	1	0	0	7	2

Green		CALORIES	PROTEIN/ GM	CARBS/ GM	TOT. FAT/ GM	SAT. FAT/ GM	CHOL/ MG	FIBRE/ GM	SODIUM/ MG
p.41	Belgian endive with blue cheese & walnuts	321	10	7	30	8	21	3	688
p.41	Spring onions with anchovy sauce	112	4	5	9	1	10	2	485
p.42	Grilled fish tacos with green cabbage salad	538	24	39	34	5	56	11	995
p.45	Trout & green pear salad	353	32	14	18	3	86	3	82
p.45	Grilled halibut with limes	373	27	4	27	5	84	1	171
p.48	Chicken, avocado & spinach salad	525	41	20	33	5	96	9	322
p.48	Green & yellow beans with almonds	200	6	12	16	2	0	6	293
p.51	Lamb chops with rocket pesto	421	24	3	35	6	85	1	350
p.51	Broccoli gratin	301	11	20	21	5	17	3	537
p.52	Grilled apple pancakes	244	5	43	7	4	69	2	340

White & tan		CALORIES	PROTEIN/ GM	CARBS/ GM	TOT. FAT/ GM	SAT. FAT/ GM	CHOL/ MG	FIBRE/ GM	SODIUM/ MG
p.59	Mushroom bruschetta	316	12	46	9	2	6	6	777
p.59	Mustard-honey leeks	165	1	9	14	2	0	1	74
p.60	Turkey sandwiches with sweet onions	415	34	32	17	3	56	2	858
p.60	Grilled white corn salad	139	3	22	6	1	0	3	211
p.63	Grilled lobster tails with white corn salsa	264	9	25	17	4	23	6	141
p.66	Cuban-style pork & plantains	452	32	33	22	7	86	2	362
p.69	White aubergine & spring onion salad	120	2	9	9	1	0	4	6
p.69	Grilled fennel with Indian spices	113	4	12	6	1	2	4	229
p.70	White nectarine kebabs	94	2	23	0	0	0	3	1

Yellow & orange		CALORIES	PROTEIN/ GM	CARBS/ GM	TOT. FAT/ GM	SAT. FAT/ GM	CHOL/ MG	FIBRE/ GM	SODIUM/ MG
p.77	Yellow tomatoes with mint & pecorino	92	5	9	5	2	6	2	159
p.77	Grilled pumpkin with pumpkin seed dressing	112	2	7	9	1	0	1	2
p.78	Grilled salmon, potato & corn salad	558	36	32	32	5	90	4	96
p.81	Grilled duck breast with papaya	423	43	14	21	5	231	3	308
p.84	Grilled snapper & mandarin salad	246	36	16	5	1	60	4	308
p.84	Swordfish with mango salsa	217	32	11	5	1	124	1	236
p.87	Japanese-style grilled sweet potatoes	129	2	18	6	1	0	3	104
p.87	Grilled squash salad	115	3	9	8	2	8	2	274
p.88	Grilled apricots with sabayon	225	4	36	8	2	205	2	10

Red		CALORIES	PROTEIN/ GM	CARBS/ GM	TOT. FAT/ GM	SAT. FAT/ GM	CHOL/ MG	FIBRE/ GM	SODIUM/ MG
p.95	Grilled radicchio	131	4	7	10	3	6	1	172
p.95	Liver & onion bruschetta	360	21	39	12	3	201	4	542
p.96	Grilled calamari with about ⅓ cup Romesco sauce per serving	284	27	19	12	1	330	3	125
p.99	Prawns with watermelon, feta & mint	272	28	11	13	5	198	1	633
p.99	Grilled cherry tomatoes	31	1	3	2	0	0	1	101
p.102	Lamb kebabs with blood orange salad	377	23	26	21	5	74	10	214
p.105	Veal chops with red plum sauce	301	33	11	13	4	131	1	555
p.105	Grilled chicken with cherry salsa	230	29	12	7	1	78	1	217
p.106	Caramelised red pears with cinnamon	309	1	68	1	1	3	7	6
p.106	Grilled grapes in yoghurt & sour cream	237	3	45	6	4	19	1	45

Brown		CALORIES	PROTEIN/ GM	CARBS/ GM	TOT. FAT/ GM	SAT. FAT/ GM	CHOL/ MG	FIBRE/ GM	SODIUM/ MG
p.113	Grilled polenta with mushroom ragout	287	10	23	18	8	29	5	1258
p.114	Chicken thighs with butter bean puree	632	40	25	40	13	168	6	1322
p.117	Grilled tuna with cannellini bean salad	570	48	33	26	4	65	9	1046
p.120	Grilled pepper & quinoa salad	161	5	27	4	1	0	4	397
p.123	Bulgur salad with courgette, asparagus & spring onions	240	8	36	9	1	0	9	515
p.124	Grilled bananas with nuts & chocolate	227	3	35	11	4	0	5	1

Glossary

anchovies: These tiny Mediterranean fish are high in heart-healthy omega-3 fatty acids. They are generally boned, cured, packed in oil and sold in small tins or jars.

apples: The major portion of the apple's nutrition is in its skin, which contains the flavonoid quercetin, an antioxidant that fights viruses and allergies and is thought to be an anticarcinogen. Apple flesh is an important source of pectin, a fibre that lowers cholesterol.

apricots: The apricot's colour is due to the pigments beta-carotene and lycopene, which promote eye health and heart health, lower the risk of some cancers and strengthen the immune system. Apricots are also high in vitamin C, potassium and fibre.

artichokes: The artichoke's fleshy heart provides a complex of heart-healthy phyto-chemicals, including cynarin; it also contains chlorophyll and beta-carotene and provides a wide range of vitamins and minerals.

asparagus: This vegetable is one of the best sources of folate, a B vitamin that helps fight heart disease and keeps the female reproductive system healthy. It is also rich in phytochemicals, depending on its colour (it comes in green, white and purple).

aubergines: The purple skin of the familiar globe aubergine is rich in heart- and brain-healthy anthocyanins, while its flesh contains saponins, antioxidants that help to lower cholesterol levels. Other varieties may be slightly smaller and have lavender, white, rose, green or variegated skin. The colour of the skin does not determine the flavour.

avocados: Technically a fruit, the avocado is high in fat, but most of it is monounsaturated, which helps to lower cholesterol. It also contains beta-sitosterol, a plant cholesterol that lowers cholesterol as well and may prevent the growth of cancer cells. Avocados are high in vitamins and minerals, especially vitamins A, C, B_6, folate and potassium.

bananas: Bananas are particularly high in potassium, which balances sodium, helps regulate blood pressure and may reduce arterial plaque formation. Potassium also helps to prevent strokes by lowering platelet activity and reducing blood clots. Bananas are also high in vitamins C and B_6 and contain a kind of fibre that may protect against colon cancer.

basil: Traditionally used in kitchens throughout the Mediterranean and in Southeast Asia, basil is one of the world's best-loved herbs and is a source of green phytonutrients. Also related to mint, basil tastes faintly of anise and cloves. Italian cooks use it in pesto and often pair it with tomatoes. In Thailand and Vietnam, basil is often combined with fresh mint for seasoning stir-fries, curries and salads.

beans, broad: A type of shell bean also known as fava beans, fresh broad beans are in season only in spring. The beans contain folate, vitamin B_1, zinc and protein. They are also a source of levodopa, a chemical known to fight Parkinson's disease.

beans, butter: These are high in fibre and a good source of protein. They contain beneficial minerals such as molybdenum, which helps your body detoxify sulfites; magnesium; and folic acid.

beans, cannellini: These ivory-colored kidney beans, used in Italian cooking, have a buttery texture and a delicate taste.

beans, kidney: Shaped like the organ that gives them their name, red kidney beans are meaty and have a more assertive flavour than cannellini beans.

beans, navy: Also called haricot beans, these small, dried beans are high in fibre and protein and contain folic acid and vitamin B_1. They are also good sources of magnesium and potassium, important minerals for heart health, and iron, which gives you energy.

beans, yellow wax: These edible pod beans are similar to green beans, only yellow, and contain vitamin C, iron and folate which helps prevent heart attacks.

beetroots: Red beetroots get their deep colour from the phytochemical betacyanin, which is believed to reduce tumor growth. They also contain betaine, which helps protect the heart and salicylic acid, which has anti-inflammatory properties and are especially high in folate. The phytochemicals found in golden beetroots help promote eye health and boost overall immunity.

Belgian endive: A member of the chicory family, Belgian endive is blanched (grown in darkness) to prevent it from turning green. It does contain phyto-chemicals based on the colour of the tips, purple or green.

blackberries: Rich in purple antioxidants, these sweet berries are also high in tannins, which tighten tissues and help fight inflammation. Their colour is due to anthoyanins which helps to lower the risk of some cancers.

blueberries: These native American berries are high in antioxidant and anti-inflammatory compounds and they are considered "brain food": they contain a range of anthocyanins, which are thought to help fight cancer and have antiageing capabilities. Blueberries are available fresh, dried and frozen.

broccoli: Extremely high in vitamin C (60 g/2 oz provides 68 percent of the daily recommended intake) and even higher in vitamin K, broccoli also contains vitamin A and cancer-fighting phytochemicals. Broccoli sprouts also contain high levels of these compounds.

broccoli, sprouting: With its long, thin stalks and small flowering heads, broccoli rabe has an assertive, bitter flavor. It contains many of the same nutrients as broccoli.

bulgur wheat: Like other whole grains, bulgur wheat is rich in selenium, an antioxidant that is believed to fight cancer. Bulgur wheat kernels have been steamed, dried and crushed, and are available in various grinds.

cabbage: The patriarch of the cruciferous vegetable family, cabbage is high in vitamins C and K, but its real value is its concentration of isothiocyanates, powerful cancer-fighting compounds. Red purple cabbage contains more vitamin C than green cabbage along with the antioxidant anthocyanin.

Cajun spice mix: This potent blend of spices, including ground red chilli, may contain garlic, paprika, sage and mustard.

caper berries: The fruit of the same shrub that produces capers. Olive-shaped with long stems, caper berries are pickled or salted, and like capers, they must be rinsed before use.

capers: A Mediterranean shrub is the source of these small unopened flower buds. The buds are bitter when raw; once they are dried and packed in brine or salt, they are used to add a pleasantly pungent flavour to a variety of dishes. Capers should be rinsed before use to remove excess brine or salt.

carrots: One carrot provides a whopping 330 percent of the daily recommended intake of vitamin A, which is the source of its fame as a protector of eye health. Carrots are also high in fibre and the bioflavonoids and carotenoids that lower the risk of some cancers, protect the heart and boost immunity. Maroon and purple carrots are colourful alternatives to the common orange carrot, offering different phytochemical benefits, and these colours of carrot are becoming more widely available.

celery: Like other green vegetables, celery promotes eye health, strengthens the immune system and helps build strong bones and teeth. It is also high in fibre.

cheese, blue: These cheeses are inoculated with the spores of special moulds to develop a fine network of blue veins for a strong, sharp, peppery flavour and a crumbly texture. Most blue cheeses can be crumbled, diced, spread or sliced. Depending on the cheese's moisture content, however, some hold their shape when sliced better than others.

cheese, feta: Young cheese traditionally made from sheep's milk and used in Greek cuisine. It is known for its crumbly texture; some versions are also creamy. Feta's saltiness is heightened by the brine in which the cheese is pickled. Feta is also produced from cow's or goat's milk. Reduced-fat feta is also available.

cheese, pecorino: A little of this pleasantly salty, firm Italian sheep's milk cheese goes a long way, making it an excellent choice for grating or shaving over dishes to add flavour.

cheese, ricotta: This mild, soft cheese, sold in tubs, is made by heating the whey left over from making other types of cheese, often mozzarella. It can be served in sweet or savoury preparations and is available in low-fat versions.

cherries: Tart red and sweet dark red cherries derive their colour from anthocyanin pigments and other antioxidants, which help protect the heart and brain, lower the risk of some cancers and are powerful anti-inflammatories. Both sweet and tart cherries also contain a terpenoid that appears to prevent the growth of tumours.

chickpeas: These crumpled-looking dried beans are meaty and hearty-flavoured when cooked. They are popular in soups and purées and are the basis for hummus, the Middle Eastern dip.

chillis: All chillis contain the phytochemical capsaicin, which gives them their hot taste and also acts as a cancer fighter. Although usually eaten only in small amounts, they are nutrient rich, containing vitamins A, C, and E, along with folic acid and potassium.

chilli sauce, Thai sweet: A purée of chillis with a sweet flavour in addition to heat, this sauce is often used to season prawn and noodle dishes in Southeast Asia. It is commonly used as a condiment.

Chinese five-spice powder: This distinctive spice blend varies in its make-up, but usually contains cloves, fennel seeds, star anise, cinnamon, Sichuan peppercorns and sometimes ginger.

chives: These slender, bright green stems are used to give an onionlike flavour without the bite. The grasslike leaves can be snipped and scattered over scrambled eggs, stews, salads, soups, tomatoes or any dish that would benefit from a boost of mild oniony flavour. Chives do not take well to long cooking—they lose flavour, colour and crispness.

coriander: Also called Chinese parsley, coriander is a distinctively flavoured herb with legions of loyal followers. Used extensively in the cuisines of India, Egypt, Thailand, Vietnam and China, coriander asserts itself with a flavour that can't be missed. It is best used fresh and added at the end of cooking.

corn: Corn holds a wealth of vitamins, minerals, protein and fibre. Yellow corn is given its colour by carotenoids that not only fight heart disease and cancer, but also protect against macular degeneration.

courgettes: Most of the courgettes nutrients are found in its skin, which contains phytochemicals that strengthen the eyes, bones and teeth; help to boost immunity; and lower the risk of some cancers.

cucumbers: A member of the gourd family, the phytochemically rich skin of cucumbers can be eaten. Cucumbers have been found to be one of the best sources of cancer-fighting phytochemicals.

dill: The fine, feathery leaves of this herb have a distinct aromatic flavor. Dill is used in savoury pastries, baked vegetables and of course, in the making and jarring of pickles.

fennel: Mild and sweet with an anise-like flavour, this pale green bulb contains the phyto-nutrient anethole, which has been found in some studies to reduce inflammation and prevent cancer. Fennel is also a good source of antioxidants, fibre and vitamin C.

fennel seeds: The seed of the common fennel has a liquorice-like flavour and may be used ground or whole in savoury dishes such as bouillabaisse, sausage and pork stews and roasts. It is also used in some breads and desserts and to flavour liqueurs.

figs: Whether fresh (available in summer and early autumn) or dried, figs provide phosphorus, calcium and iron.

fish sauce: Made from salted, fermented fish, often anchovies, this salty-tart Southeast Asian sauce adds to countless dishes a depth of flavour that regular salt can't match.

garam masala: In India, each region or cook has a different recipe for this aromatic blend of roasted, ground spices. It commonly includes cumin, fennel, cardamom, cloves, cinnamon, nutmeg, ginger, coriander and turmeric, the source of its warm yellow colour.

garlic: Unusually rich in antioxidants and anti-inflammatories, garlic forms organosulfur compounds when chopped, crushed or sliced. This helps lower blood pressure, slow clotting and promote heart health.

ginger: Prized in Chinese cuisine for its culinary and medicinal uses, ginger aids digestion and lowers cholesterol. It contains both antioxidant and anti-microbial compounds.

grapes: Dark purple grapes are very high in antioxidants, making them an important heart-healthy food. Red table grapes also promote heart health and immunity, and green grapes can promote eye health.

green beans: Providing both vitamins A and C, green beans also protect eye health because of their lutein content.

kirsch: Named for the German word for "cherry", this dry, clear brandy is made from distilled fermented cherry juice and stones.

lamb's lettuce: It appears in early spring. This green is delicate and mild, with oval leaves that grow in small, loose bunches. Like other dark greens, it contains vitamin C, beta-carotene, and folic acid, but also includes vitamin B_9, which combats stress and fatigue.

leeks: By virtue of their membership in the onion family, leeks contain organosulfur compounds, which are thought to fight cancer and heart disease. They also help improve the body's good-bad cholesterol ratio.

lemons: High in vitamin C, lemons are a flavour enhancer; add lemon juice to raw and cooked fruits and use it to replace salt at the table for vegetables and fish.

lettuces: The many types of lettuce can be divided into four major groups: butterhead, crisphead, leaf and cos (romaine). Most lettuces are high in vitamins A and C; they also provide calcium and iron. The darker the green of the lettuce, the higher the level of its beneficial phytochemicals, which include the eye-protectant lutein.

limes: High in vitamin C, like all citrus fruits, lime juice also contains lutein, which benefits eye health. The juice is available in bottles.

mangetouts: Once both tips are pinched off, the thin, delicate mangetout is completely edible, either raw or cooked. It provides both calcium and iron.

mango: Rich in beta-carotene, vitamin C and many other protective phytochemicals, mangoes are also a low-fat source of vitamin E. Select ripe mangoes that are aromatic at their stem end and give slightly when gentle pressure is applied.

melons: Higher in healthful nutrients than any other melon, the cantaloupe is also rich in vitamins A and C and potassium. It is heart healthy and helps to lower the risk of cancer, thanks to its beta-carotene content. A wide variety of other orange-fleshed melons are also available. Green-fleshed honeydew melons contain cancer-fighting phytochemicals as well.

mint: A refreshing herb available in many varieties, with spearmint the most common. Used fresh to flavour a broad range of savoury preparations, including spring lamb, poultry and vegetables, or to decorate desserts.

miso: A staple in Japan, this fermented soybean paste has a salty earthy flavor and is high in the vitamin B_{12} and rich in enzymes and digestive aids. White (light or yellow) miso and darker red miso are available.

mushrooms: Not vegetables or fruits but fungi, mushrooms come in a variety of forms and are available both wild and cultivated. They are rich in riboflavin, niacin and pantothenic acid, all B-complex vitamins and also contain the valuable minerals copper and selenium.

nectarines: The nectarine, relative of the peach, has the advantage of an edible skin that contains many of its phytochemicals. Yellow nectarines contain beta-carotene, while the pink-skinned, white-fleshed variety has its own group of beneficial compounds.

nuts: High in fibre, nuts also contain folate, riboflavin and magnesium. They are high in beneficial omega-3 fatty acids and vitamin E, an antioxidant that protects brain cells, promotes heart health and lowers "bad" LDL cholesterol.

olives: One of the worlds most reliable crops, olives have helped sustain people in the Mediterranean for thousands of years. Too bitter to eat when fresh, olives are either pressed to make oil, which is prized for its high levels of vitamin E and heart-healthy monounsaturated fats, or cured. Deep purple kalamata olives contain powerful antioxidants.

onions: All onions contain organosulfur compounds that are thought to fight cancer and to promote heart health. Yellow and red onions also contain quercetin, which boosts these actions, while red onions have the added benefit of the antioxidant anthocyanin.

oranges: Famed for their high vitamin C content, oranges are also high in folate and potassium. They also provide limonoids and flavonoids, two disease-fighting antioxidants. Blood oranges have dramatic red flesh and juice, as well as a flavour reminiscent of berries. Less acidic and smaller than other oranges, mandarin oranges are often called tangerines, which are just one type. Popular varieties include Satsuma and Clementine.

oyster sauce: This thick dark brown, smoky-sweet sauce is made from oyster extracts and seasonings, including soy sauce. It is commonly used in Cantonese cuisine and adds depth of flavour to marinades.

papaya: This tropical fruit was native to Central America, but is now cultivated from Hawaii to South Africa to the Philippines. Its sweet yellow- to orange-coloured flesh contains vitamins A and C, folic acid, potassium and papain, an enzyme that helps with digestion.

paprika: Made from ground dried red pimento peppers, the best paprikas come from Hungary and Spain. Most paprikas are mild and sweet, although you can find hot paprika as well. Seek out smoked Spanish pimentòn for added depth of flavour.

peaches: While the fruit's fuzzy skin is often not eaten, yellow or white peach flesh contains the vitamins A and C. Peaches are available fresh, dried and tinned.

peanuts: Although they are not truly nuts, but legumes, peanuts are high in fat. They are a good source of protein, but they should be eaten in small amounts. Like most nuts, the fat they contain is largely monounsaturated.

pears: The beneficial pigments of pears are concentrated in their skin; as the skin is quite thin (except in the tan-skinned varieties), they can be eaten unpeeled, whether raw or cooked. The flesh contains vitamin A, as well as some phosphorus.

peas: Also called green peas, these should be eaten soon after picking; they are also available frozen. They provide niacin and iron, along with vitamins A and C.

peas, sugar snap: A cross between the pea and the mangetout, sugar snaps resemble the former but are entirely edible either cooked or raw. They provide vitamins A and C, along with folate, iron, phosphorus and thiamin.

peppers: All peppers are high in cancer fighting phytochemicals; the various compounds that give them their different colours (green, yellow, orange and red) also promote eye health; the antioxidants in purple peppers aid memory function and promote healthy ageing. Red peppers are high in vitamin C.

pineapples: The pineapple's sweet, juicy flesh provides manganese, vitamins A and C and bromelain, an antiflammatory enzyme that is also a digestive aid.

pine nuts: Delicate, buttery pine nuts contain both iron and thiamin. They are a favoured garnish for salads and cooked foods. Toasting the nuts brings out their flavour.

plantains: A plantain tastes like a less sweet, blander version of the banana. Its high starch content allows it to be cooked in many ways, and its neutral flavour allows it to pair well with a variety of ingredients.

plums: The edible skin of the plum, which comes in a variety of colours, contains most of its phytochemicals, although the yellow, purple or red flesh also contains beneficial compounds. A good source of vitamin C, plums are one of the most healthy fruits. When they are not in season, enjoy them as prunes, their dried form.

polenta: Although polenta may be made from other dried grains or white corn, usually it is coarsely or finely ground yellow cornmeal. Only stone-ground cornmeal is whole grain; store it in an airtight container in the refrigerator.

pomelos: Similar to grapefruit and used in many of the same ways, pomelos have very thick skin ranging in colour from yellow to beige to pink. Like other citrus, they are a good source of potassium and vitamin C.

potatoes: The deeper the colour of its pigment, the more healthy phytochemicals a potato possesses, but all potatoes are extremely rich in vitamins and minerals if eaten with the skin; they are also high in fibre. Be sure to buy organic potatoes if you plan to eat the skins.

prunes: These dried prune plums, now also called dried plums, are rich in vitamin A, potassium and fibre. They are higher in anti-oxidants than any other fruit or vegetable, making them the top antiageing food.

pumpkins: The flesh of the pumpkin is nutrient rich with vitamin A and carotenoids, specifically the cancer-fighters alpha- and beta-carotene and lutein.

pumpkin seeds: High in fibre, protein and various minerals, pumpkin seeds also contain beta-sisterol, which lowers cholesterol and slows the growth of abnormal cells. Look for them in natural foods stores.

quinoa: An ancient Incan grain, quinoa is higher in protein than all other grains, and its protein is complete. It is also rich in nutrients and unsaturated fat.

radicchio: A red-leafed member of the chicory family, radicchio has an assertive, bitter flavour, and provides beneficial antioxidants such as anthocyanins and lycopene. Radicchio may be eaten raw, grilled, baked or sautéed.

raisins: Antioxidant rich, raisins are also high in vitamins, minerals and fibre. Both dark raisins and sultanas start as green grapes, but sultanas are treated with sulfur dioxide to prevent oxidation.

raspberries: Red raspberries have more fibre than most other fruits; they are also high in vitamin C and folate and extremely high in cancer-fighting antioxidants. Golden raspberries are much less common, but they contain heart- and eye-healthy bioflavonoids. Although fresh raspberries can be a bit fragile, frozen unsweetened raspberries retain their flavour and are available year-round.

rice, brown: This whole grain retains its bran covering, making it high in fibre. Brown rice is available in long-, medium- and short-grain varieties. Like other whole grains, it is high in fibre and selenium; because the bran can become rancid at room temperature, brown rice should be kept refrigerated.

rocket: A peppery green, rocket is eaten both cooked and raw. It is a good source of iron and vitamins A and C and contains lutein, which protects eye health.

rosemary: Used fresh or dried, this Mediterranean herb has a strong, fragrant flavour well suited to meats, poultry, seafood and vegetables. It is a particularly good complement to roasted chicken and lamb.

rosewater: Used as a flavouring and tea ingredient in the Middle East, India and China, rosewater smells like its name and has a distinctive flavour. It is made from distilled rose petals.

sake: This alcoholic Japanese beverage is made from fermented rice and is somewhat similar to beer in the way it is made. It is enjoyed as a beverage and also used as a seasoning in cooking.

sesame oil: Rich, nutty, amber-colored dark Asian sesame oil is pressed from toasted sesame seeds and is most often used in small amounts as a flavouring. Lighter types of sesame oil have a subtler flavour and can be used for dressings and frying. Both are high in polyunsaturated fats and cholesterol-lowering vitamin E.

sesame seeds: Flat and minute, sesame seeds come in several colours, but are most commonly light ivory. They are rich in manganese, copper and calcium, and also contain cholesterol-lowering lignans. Because they have a high oil content, they should be kept refrigerated. Toasting them briefly in a dry frying pan over medium heat brings out their nutty flavour.

shallots: Another onion family member, the shallot contains the same heart-healthy organosulfides as its relatives. It is milder in taste and more convenient to use in small amounts than the onion.

soft wheat flour: Low in protein and high in starch, this flour is milled from soft wheat to which cornflour is added. Finer than plain flour, it gives baked goods a light crumb.

spinach: High in a multitude of nutrients, from vitamins A, C, and K to folate and potassium, spinach is also one of the best sources of lutein, the carotenoid that prevents macular degeneration.

spring onions: Like all onions, spring onions contain organosulfur compounds, which are thought to protect the heart and improve the good/bad cholesterol ratio.

squash, summer: Most of the squash's nutrients are contained in its bright, edible yellow skin. It is a good source of manganese, as well as the beneficial carotenoids that give it its sunny colour.

squash, winter: The dense, meaty flesh of winter squashes is rich with vitamins A and C, folate, manganese and potassium, as well as heart-protective and cancer-fighting carotenoids.

star anise: A seed-bearing pod from a Chinese evergreen tree, this unique spice has a faint liquorice taste and flavours teas and savoury dishes throughout Asia.

strawberries: Rich in antioxidant content, partly due to their anthocyanin pigments, strawberries are also extremely high in vitamin C. Because of these compounds, as well as their phenolic acids, these berries are thought to be important cancer-fighters.

sugar, caster: This is the finely ground form of granulated sugar. It dissolves rapidly.

sweet potatoes: The most commonly available of these root vegetables are a pale yellow variety and a dark orange one often erroneously referred to as a yam. Both are high in fibre, vitamins A and C and a host of other vitamins and minerals, as well as more beta-carotene than any other vegetable.

tahini: A paste made from ground sesame seeds, tahini has a rich, creamy, concentrated flavour. It is most popular as an essential ingredient in such Mediterranean spreads as hummus and baba ghanoush and provides many of the same benefits as sesame oil.

tomatillos: Sometimes called Mexican green tomatoes, tomatillos are firmer and less juicy than tomatoes and grow to ripeness inside a pale-green papery sheath. Used both raw and cooked, they are an essential sweet-sour ingredient in many Mexican green sauces. Look for fresh or tinned tomatillos in well-stocked supermarkets.

tomatoes: Not only are tomatoes high in vitamin C, they are also high in fibre and have good amounts of other vitamins and minerals. Red tomatoes also contain lycopene, which lowers cancer risk. Yellow, green and purple tomatoes each offer antioxidants. The body absorbs the antioxidant better when tomatoes are cooked.

vinegar: Many types are available, made from a variety of red or white wines or, like cider vinegar and rice vinegar, from fruits and grains. Vinegars are further seasoned by infusing them with fresh herbs, fruit, garlic or other flavoursome ingredients, including sugar, which is used in the seasoned

rice vinegar that flavours sushi rice.

watercress: This spicy green is, surprisingly, a cruciferous vegetable. It contains good amounts of vitamins A and C. The peppery taste of watercress is due to a certain isothio-cyanate that has shown the potential to help combat lung cancer.

watermelon: Despite its high water content, this melon provides vitamins A and C, along with the anthocyanins that give it its colour.

wine: The colours of red and rosé wines are due to the skins of the purple grapes used to make the wines; red wine has more beneficial flavonoids than grape juice. These phytochemicals have been shown to help increase "good" HDL cholesterol.

yoghurt: The bacterial cultures in yoghurt are prized as an aid in digestion. Like the milk it is made from, yoghurt can be full fat, low fat or skimmed.

Index

A

Almonds
    Chicken, Avocado & Spinach Salad, 48
    Green & Yellow Beans with Almonds, 48
    Romesco Sauce, 96
Anchovies, 134
    Spring Onions with Anchovy Sauce, 41
Apples, 134
    Crisp Green Apple & Celery Salad, 46
    Grilled Apple Pancakes, 52
Apricots, 134
    Grilled Apricots with Sabayon, 88
Artichokes, 134
    Grilled Artichoke Salad, 46
Asparagus, 134
    Bulgur Salad with Courgettes, Asparagus,
        & Spring Onions, 123
    Grilled Salmon with Purple Asparagus
        Slaw, 30
Aubergines, 136
    Chicken, Aubergine & Tomato Salad, 33
    Grilled Aubergine & Feta Cheese Rolls, 23
    White Aubergine & Spring Onion Salad, 66
Avocados, 134
    Chicken, Avocado & Spinach Salad, 48

B

Bacon-Wrapped Prunes, 28
Bananas, 134
    Grilled Bananas with Nuts & Chocolate, 124
    Grilled Berry Parcels, 34
Beans, 134, 136. *See also* Chickpeas
    Chicken Thighs with Butter Bean Purée, 114
    Green & Yellow Beans with Almonds, 48
    Grilled Broad Beans, 47
    Grilled Tuna with Cannellini Bean Salad, 117
    Prawns, Beans, & Tomatoes, 119
    Red Kidney Bean Quesadillas, 119
Beetroots, 134
    Sweet & Sour Beetroots, 100
Belgian endive, 134
    Belgian Endive with Blue Cheese

    & Walnuts, 41
    Fig & Purple Endive Salad, 27
Berries, 134–35, 138, 139
    Grilled Berry Parcels, 34
Blue recipes. *See* Purple & blue recipes
Broccoli, 135
    Broccoli Gratin, 51
Broccoli, sprouting, 135
Brown recipes, 13, 110, 133
    Grilled Bananas with Nuts & Chocolate, 124
    Grilled Pepper & Quinoa Salad, 120
    Grilled Polenta with Mushroom Ragout, 113
    Grilled Rice Patties with Asian Flavours, 118
    Grilled Tuna with Cannellini Bean Salad, 117
    Bulgur Salad with Courgettes, Asparagus
        & Spring Onions, 123
    Chicken Thighs with Butter Bean Purée, 114
    Chickpeas with Baby Spinach, 119
    Prawns, Beans & Tomatoes, 119
    Red Kidney Bean Quesadillas, 119
Bruschetta
    Liver & Onion Bruschetta, 95
    Mushroom Bruschetta, 59
Bulgur wheat, 135
    Bulgur Salad with Courgettes, Asparagus
        & Spring Onions, 123

C

Cabbage, 135
    Grilled Fish Tacos with Green
        Cabbage Salad, 42
    Grilled Purple Cabbage, 29
Cajun spice mix, 135
Cake flour, 135
Calamari, Grilled, 96
Caperberries, 135
Capers, 135
Carbohydrates, 10, 126
Carrots, 135
    Moroccan Carrot Salad, 82
Celery, 135
    Crisp Green Apple & Celery Salad, 46
Cheese, 17, 135

    Belgian Endive with Blue Cheese
        & Walnuts, 41
    Broccoli Gratin, 51
    Chicken Thighs with Butter Bean Purée, 114
    Figs with Ricotta, 29
    Grilled Squash Salad, 87
    Grilled Aubergine & Feta Cheese Rolls, 23
    Grilled Pizzas with Purple Potatoes
        & Onions, 24
    Grilled Polenta with Mushroom
        Ragout, 113
    Prawns with Watermelon, Feta & Mint, 99
    Red Kidney Bean Quesadillas, 119
    Yellow Tomatoes with Mint & Pecorino, 77
Cherries, 135
    Chicken with Cherry Salsa, 105
Chicken
    Chicken & Fig Kebabs, 33
    Chicken, Avocado & Spinach Salad, 48
    Chicken, Aubergine & Tomato Salad, 33
    Chicken Thighs with Butter Bean Purée, 114
    Chicken with Cherry Salsa, 105
Chickpeas, 135
    Bulgur Salad with Courgettes, Asparagus
        & Spring Onions, 123
    Chickpeas with Baby Spinach, 119
Chillis, 135
    Grilled Chilli Sauce, 100
    sauce, Thai sweet, 135
Chives, 135–36
Chocolate, Grilled Bananas with Nuts &, 124
Coriander, 136
Corn, 136
    Grilled Lobster Tails with Corn Salsa, 63
    Grilled Salmon, Yellow Potato,
        & Corn Salad, 78
    Grilled White Corn Salad, 60
    Grilled White Corn with Herb Butter, 64
Courgettes, 139
    Bulgur Salad with Courgettes, Asparagus
        & Spring Onions, 123
Couscous, Israeli, 136
Cuban-Style Pork & Plantains, 69

Cucumbers, 136

D
Dill, 136
Duck Breast, Grilled, with Papaya, 81

F
Fats, 10, 17, 127
Fennel, 136
   Grilled Fennel with Indian Spices, 66
Fennel seeds, 136
Fibre, 13
Figs, 136
   Chicken & Fig Kebabs, 33
   Fig & Purple Endive Salad, 27
Fish. *See also* Anchovies; Halibut; Salmon
   Grilled Snapper & Mandarin Salad, 84
   Grilled Tuna with Cannellini Bean Salad, 117
   Swordfish with Mango Salsa, 84
   Trout & Green Pear Salad, 45
Fish sauce, 136
Five-spice powder, 135
Fresh Ideas
   Bacon-Wrapped Prunes, 28
   Chickpeas with Baby Spinach, 119
   Crisp Green Apple & Celery Salad, 46
   Figs with Ricotta, 29
   Grilled Artichoke Salad, 46
   Grilled Chilli Sauce, 100
   Grilled Favas, 47
   Grilled Parsnip crisps with Lemon
     & Honey, 65
   Grilled Pineapple, 83
   Grilled Pomelo, 83
   Grilled Purple Cabbage, 29
   Grilled Blue Potatoes, 28
   Grilled Red Peppers, 101
   Grilled Rice Patties with Asian Flavours, 118
   Grilled Shallots, 64
   Grilled White Corn with Herb Butter, 64
   Honeydew Prosciutto Wraps, 47
   Moroccan Carrot Salad, 82
   Orange Gazpacho, 82
   Pesto Mushrooms, 65
   Prawns, Beans & Tomatoes, 119
   Red Kidney Bean Quesadillas, 119

   Red Onions with Fennel, 101
   Sweet & Sour Beetroots, 100
Fruits, 8–9, 11, 12, 16. *See also individual fruits*

G
Garam masala, 136
Garlic, 136
Gazpacho, Orange, 83
Ginger, 136
   Ginger Sauce, 70
Grains, 9, 11, 13
Grapes, 136
   Grilled Grapes in Yoghurt & Sour Cream, 106
   Halibut & Purple Grapes, 27
Green recipes, 38, 131
   Belgian Endive with Blue Cheese
     & Walnuts, 41
   Broccoli Gratin, 51
   Chicken, Avocado & Spinach Salad, 48
   Crisp Green Apple & Celery Salad, 46
   Green & Yellow Beans with Almonds, 48
   Grilled Apple Hotcakes, 52
   Grilled Artichoke Salad, 46
   Grilled Favas, 47
   Grilled Fish Tacos with Green Cabbage
     Salad, 42
   Grilled Halibut with Limes, 45
   Honeydew Prosciutto Wraps, 47
   Lamb Chops with Rocket Pesto, 51
   Spring Onions with Anchovy Sauce, 41
   Trout & Green Pear Salad, 45
Grilling tips, 14–15

H
Halibut
   Grilled Fish Tacos with Green
     Cabbage Salad, 42
   Grilled Halibut with Limes, 45
   Halibut & Purple Grapes, 27
Herbs, 17. *See also individual herbs*

J-K
Japanese-Style Grilled Sweet Potatoes, 87
Kirsch, 136

L
Lamb

Lamb Chops with Rocket Pesto, 51
   Lamb Kebabs with Blood Orange Salad, 102
Lamb's Lettuce, 136–37
Leeks, 136
   Mustard-Honey Leeks, 59
Legumes, 9, 11, 13. *See also individual legumes*
Lemons, 136
Lettuces, 136
Limes, 136
   Grilled Halibut with Limes, 45
Liver & Onion Bruschetta, 95
Lobster, 136
   Grilled Lobster Tails with Corn Salsa, 63

M
Mangoes, 137
   Swordfish with Mango Salsa, 84
Meal planning, 16–17
Meat, 16–17. *See also individual meats*
Melons, 137, 139
   Honeydew Prosciutto Wraps, 47
   Prawns with Watermelon, Feta & Mint, 99
Minerals, 10–11, 129
Mint, 137
Miso, 137
Moroccan Carrot Salad, 82
Mushrooms, 137
   Grilled Polenta with Mushroom Ragout, 113
   Mushroom Bruschetta, 59
   Pesto Mushrooms, 65

N
Nectarines, 137
   White Nectarine Kebabs, 70
Nutrition, 8–13, 126–33
Nuts, 9, 13, 137. *See also individual nuts*

O
Oils, 17
Olives, 137
Onions, 137. *See also* Spring onions
   Grilled Pizzas with Purple Potatoes
     & Onions, 24
   Liver & Onion Bruschetta, 95
   Red Onions with Fennel, 101
   Turkey Sandwiches with Sweet Onions, 60

Orange recipes. *See* Yellow & orange recipes

Oranges, 137
 Grilled Snapper & Mandarin Salad, 84
 Lamb Kebabs with Blood Orange Salad, 102

Oyster sauce, 137

P

Pancakes, Grilled Apple, 52

Papayas, 137
 Grilled Duck Breast with Papaya, 81

Paprika, 137

Parsnip Crisps, Grilled, with Lemon
 & Honey, 65

Peaches, 137

Peanuts, 137

Pears, 137
 Caramelised Red Pears, 106
 Trout & Green Pear Salad, 45

Peas, 137, 138

Pecans
 Grilled Bananas with Nuts & Chocolate, 124

Peppers, 134
 Grilled Pepper & Quinoa Salad, 120
 Grilled Red Peppers, 101
 Grilled Squash Salad, 87
 Orange Gazpacho, 82
 Romesco Sauce, 96
 Scallops with Pepper Dressing, 23

Pesto
 Pesto Mushrooms, 65
 Rocket Pesto, 51

Phytochemicals, 11, 12, 13

Pineapple, 137
 Grilled Pineapple, 83
 White Nectarine Kebabs, 70

Pine nuts, 137

Pizzas, Grilled, with Purple Potatoes
 & Onions, 24

Plantains, 138
 Cuban-Style Pork & Plantains, 69

Plums, 138
 Grilled Plums with Kirsch Cream, 34
 Veal Chops with Red Plum Sauce, 105

Polenta, 138
 Grilled Polenta with Mushroom
 Ragout, 113

Pomelos, 138
 Grilled Pomelo, 83

Pork & Plantains, Cuban-Style, 69

Potatoes, 138
 Grilled Pizzas with Purple Potatoes
 & Onions, 24
 Grilled Blue Potatoes, 28
 Grilled Salmon, Yellow Potato
 & Corn Salad, 78

Prawns
 Prawns, Beans & Tomatoes, 118
 Prawns with Watermelon, Feta & Mint, 99
 Prosciutto Wraps, Honeydew, 46

Protein, 13, 127

Prunes, 138
 Bacon-Wrapped Prunes, 28

Pumpkins & pumpkin seeds, 138
 Grilled Pumpkin with Pumpkin
 Seed Dressing, 77

Purple & blue recipes, 20, 131
 Bacon-Wrapped Prunes, 28
 Chicken & Fig Kebabs, 33
 Chicken, Aubergine & Tomato Salad, 33
 Fig and Purple Endive Salad, 27
 Figs with Ricotta, 29
 Grilled Berry Parcels, 34
 Grilled Aubergine & Feta Cheese Rolls, 23
 Grilled Blue Potatoes, 28
 Grilled Pizzas with Purple Potatoes
 & Onions, 24
 Grilled Plums with Kirsch Cream, 34
 Grilled Purple Cabbage, 29
 Grilled Salmon with Purple Asparagus
 Slaw, 30
 Halibut & Purple Grapes, 27
 Scallops with Pepper
 Dressing, 23

Q

Quesadillas, Red Kidney Bean, 119

Quinoa, 138
 Grilled Pepper & Quinoa Salad, 120

R

Radicchio, 138
 Grilled Radicchio, 95

Raisins, 138

Raspberries, 138

Red recipes, 92, 133
 Caramelised Red Pears, 106
 Chicken with Cherry Salsa, 105
 Grilled Calamari, 96
 Grilled Cherry Tomatoes, 99
 Grilled Chilli Sauce, 100
 Grilled Grapes in Yoghurt & Sour Cream, 106
 Grilled Radicchio, 95
 Grilled Red Peppers, 101
 Lamb Kebabs with Blood Orange Salad, 102
 Liver & Onion Bruschetta, 95
 Prawns with Watermelon, Feta & Mint, 99
 Red Onions with Fennel, 101
 Romesco Sauce, 96
 Sweet & Sour Beetroots, 100
 Veal Chops with Red Plum Sauce, 105

Rice, 138
 Grilled Rice Patties with Asian Flavours, 118

Rocket, 134
 Lamb Chops with Rocket Pesto, 51

Romesco Sauce, 96

Rosemary, 138

Rosewater, 138

S

Sake, 138

Salads
 Bulgur Salad with Courgettes, Asparagus,
 & Spring Onions, 123
 Chicken, Avocado & Spinach Salad, 48
 Chicken, Aubergine & Tomato Salad, 33
 Crisp Green Apple & Celery Salad, 47
 Fig & Purple Endive Salad, 27
 Grilled Artichoke Salad, 46
 Grilled Squash Salad, 87
 Grilled Fish Tacos with Green Cabbage
 Salad, 42
 Grilled Pepper & Quinoa Salad, 120
 Grilled Salmon, Yellow Potato
 & Corn Salad, 78
 Grilled Snapper & Mandarin Salad, 84
 Grilled Tuna with Cannellini Bean Salad, 117
 Grilled White Corn Salad, 60
 Lamb Kebabs with Blood Orange Salad, 102

Moroccan Carrot Salad, 82
Purple Asparagus Slaw, 30
Trout & Green Pear Salad, 45
White Aubergine & Spring Onion Salad, 66
Salmon
Grilled Salmon with Purple Asparagus
Slaw, 30
Grilled Salmon, Yellow Potato
& Corn Salad, 78
Sandwiches, Turkey, with Sweet Onions, 60
Sauces
Ginger Sauce, 70
Grilled Chilli Sauce, 100
Rocket Pesto, 51
Romesco Sauce, 96
Scallops with Pepper Dressing, 23
Seeds, 9, 13
Serving size, 130
Sesame oil, 138
Sesame seeds, 138
Shallots, 138
Grilled Shallots, 64
Slaw, Purple Asparagus, 30
Snapper, Grilled, & Mandarin Salad, 84
Spices, 17
Spinach, 138
Chicken, Avocado & Spinach Salad, 48
Chickpeas with Baby Spinach, 119
Spring onions, 136
Spring Onions with Anchovy Sauce, 41
Squash, 137–8. See also Courgette
Grilled Squash Salad, 87
Squid
Grilled Calamari, 96
Star anise, 139
Strawberries, 139
Sugar, 139
Sweet potatoes, 139
Japanese-Style Grilled Sweet Potatoes, 87
Swordfish with Mango Salsa, 84

T

Tacos, Grilled Fish, with Green
Cabbage Salad, 42
Tahini, 139
Tahini Dressing, 66

Tan recipes. See White & tan recipes
Tomatillos, 139
Tomatoes, 139
Chicken, Aubergine & Tomato Salad, 33
Grilled Cherry Tomatoes, 99
Grilled Salmon, Yellow Potato,
& Corn Salad, 78
Grilled Tuna with Cannellini Bean Salad, 117
Orange Gazpacho, 82
Prawns, Beans & Tomatoes, 118
Romesco Sauce, 96
Yellow Tomatoes with Mint & Pecorino, 77
Tortillas
Grilled Fish Tacos with Green
Cabbage Salad, 42
Red Kidney Bean Quesadillas, 119
Trout & Green Pear Salad, 45
Tuna, Grilled, with Cannellini Bean Salad, 117
Turkey Sandwiches with Sweet Onions, 60

V

Veal Chops with Red Plum Sauce, 105
Vegetables, 8–9, 11, 12, 16. See also
individual vegetables
Vinegar, 139
Vitamins, 10–11, 128

W

Walnuts
Belgian Endive with Blue Cheese
& Walnuts, 41
Grilled Polenta with Mushroom Ragout, 113
Watercress, 139
Watermelon. See Melons
White & tan recipes, 56, 132
Cuban-Style Pork & Plantains, 69
Grilled Fennel with Indian Spices, 66
Grilled Lobster Tails with Corn Salsa, 63
Grilled Parsnip Crisps with Lemon
& Honey, 65
Grilled Shallots, 64
Grilled White Corn Salad, 60
Grilled White Corn with Herb Butter, 64
Mushroom Bruschetta, 59
Mustard-Honey Leeks, 59
Pesto Mushrooms, 65

Turkey Sandwiches with Sweet Onions, 60
White Aubergine & Spring Onion Salad, 66
White Nectarine Kebabs, 70
Wine, 139

Y

Yellow & orange recipes, 74, 132
Grilled Apricots with Sabayon, 88
Grilled Squash Salad, 87
Grilled Duck Breast with Papaya, 81
Grilled Pineapple, 83
Grilled Pomelo, 83
Grilled Pumpkin with Pumpkin
Seed Dressing, 77
Grilled Salmon, Yellow Potato,
& Corn Salad, 78
Grilled Snapper & Mandarin Salad, 84
Japanese-Style Grilled Sweet Potatoes, 87
Moroccan Carrot Salad, 82
Orange Gazpacho, 82
Swordfish with Mango Salsa, 84
Yellow Tomatoes with Mint & Pecorino, 77
Yoghurt, 139

BONNIER BOOKS
Appledram Barns, Birdham Road
Chichester, West Sussex PO20 7EQ

Bonnier Books Website
www.bonnierbooks.co.uk

First published in the UK
by Bonnier Books, 2007

WELDON OWEN INC.

Chief Executive Officer John Owen

President and Chief Operating Officer Terry Newell

Chief Financial Officer Christine E. Munson

Vice President International Sales Stuart Laurence

Vice President and Creative Director Gaye Allen

Vice President and Publisher Hannah Rahill

Associate Publisher Sarah Putman Clegg

Associate Editor Lauren Higgins

Art Director and Designer Marisa Kwek

Production Director Chris Hemesath

Colour Manager Teri Bell

Production Manager Todd Rechner

Conceived and produced by Weldon Owen Inc.
814 Montgomery Street, San Francisco, CA 94133
Telephone: 415 291 0100   Fax: 415 291 8841

In collaboration with Williams-Sonoma, Inc.
3250 Van Ness Avenue, San Francisco, CA 94109

A WELDON OWEN PRODUCTION
Copyright © 2007 by Weldon Owen Inc. and Williams-Sonoma Inc.

Set in Vectora

Colour separations by Mission Productions Limited.
Printed and bound in Hong Kong by Midas Printing.

ISBN 13: 978-1-905825-23-3

ACKNOWLEDGEMENTS

Weldon Owen wishes to thank the following people for their generous support in producing this book:
Copy Editor Carrie Bradley; **Consulting Editor** Sharon Silva; **Proofreaders** Kate Washington and Lesli Neilson; **Indexer** Ken DellaPenta;
Heather Belt; Leigh Noe; Jackie Mills; and Ryan Phillips.

Additional photography by Ben Dearnley: pages 18 (top right), 54 (top left), 72 (bottom left), 90 (top right)

Annabel Langbein would like to thank the BBQ Factory, New Zealand, for kindly lending
the Brinkmann barbecue used to test these recipes.

Photographer Dan Goldberg

Photographer's Assistant Shawn Convey

Food Stylist Jen Straus

Assistant Food Stylist Max La Rivière-Hedrick

A NOTE ON WEIGHTS AND MEASURES

All recipes include metric and imperial measurements. Metric conversions are based on
a standard developed for these books and have been rounded off. Actual weights may vary.